alibris

FOGGYPAWS
835 5TH ST E
SONOMA, CA 95476
UNITED STATES

To: **ALIBRIS APEX DC 76524090-86**
APEX
800 AVONDALE AVE.
GRANDVIEW HEIGHTS, OH 43212-3473

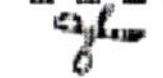

Shipping Instructions for FOGGYPA2

Print this Packing Slip and enclose inside the front cover of the book.

Please ship this item no later than Thu Jul 16, 2026.

Ship to:

ALIBRIS APEX DC 76524090-86
APEX
800 AVONDALE AVE.
GRANDVIEW HEIGHTS, OH 43212-3473
UNITED STATES

PN #	Item ID	Alibris ID	Media Type	Title / Author	Seller List Price	Order Date
76524090-86	mon0000067780	B083666256	BOOK	Second Sight: Biennial IV: San Francisco Museum of Modern Art, 21 September-16 November 1986 Beal, Graham William John	$6.31	Jul, 6 2026

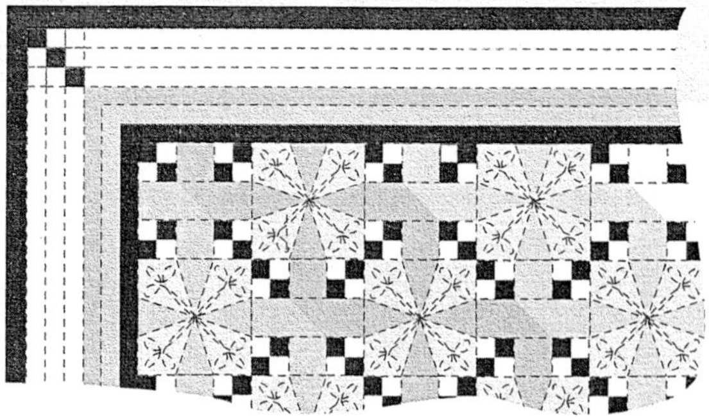

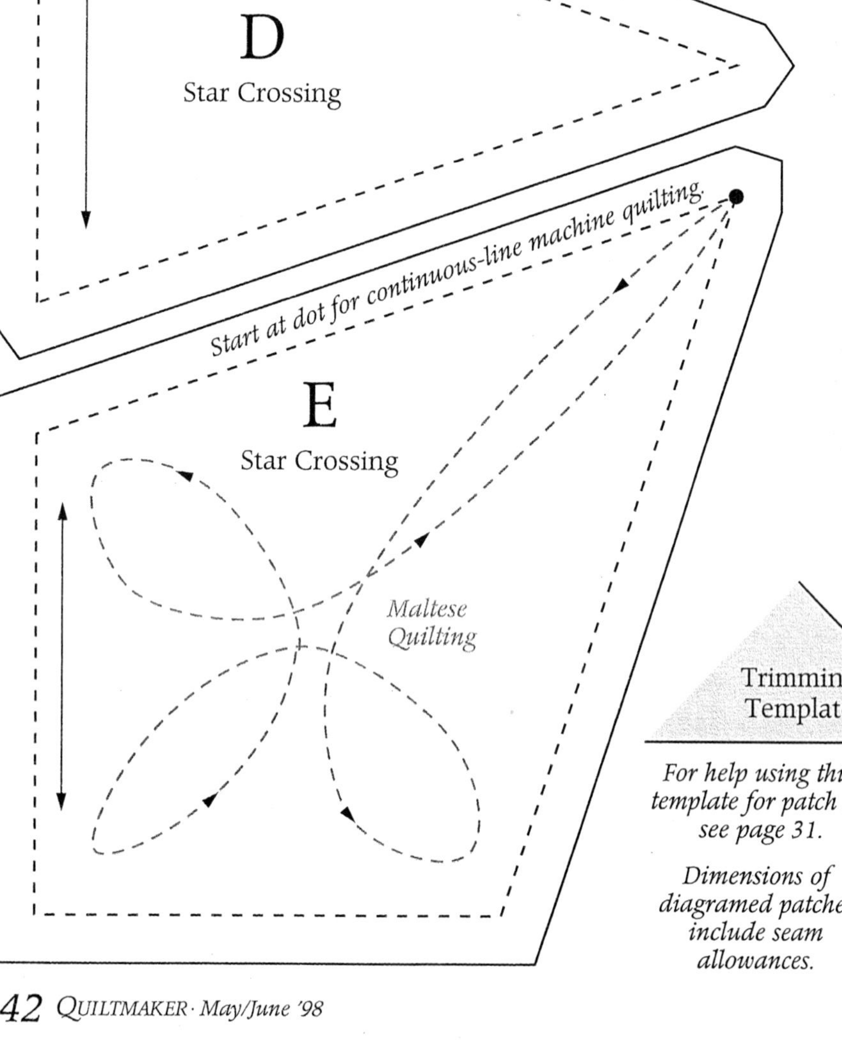
Quilting Placement

3 Completing the Quilt

Trace and mark the *Maltese Quilting* motif in the E's.

Layer and baste the lining, batting and quilt top.

Traveling across each row, quilt in the ditch the B's and D's as shown. Also quilt in the ditch the block and border seam lines. Quilt parallel lines 1¼" apart in border 4. Quilt the motifs as marked.

Join the binding strips end to end and bind the edges.

D
Star Crossing

Start at dot for continuous-line machine quilting

E
Star Crossing

Maltese Quilting

Make It Short

From the plains of North Dakota, *QM* home sewer Penny Wolf recommends shortening your stitch length when strip piecing. The shorter stitch length keeps the seams from pulling apart after the strips have been cut into units.

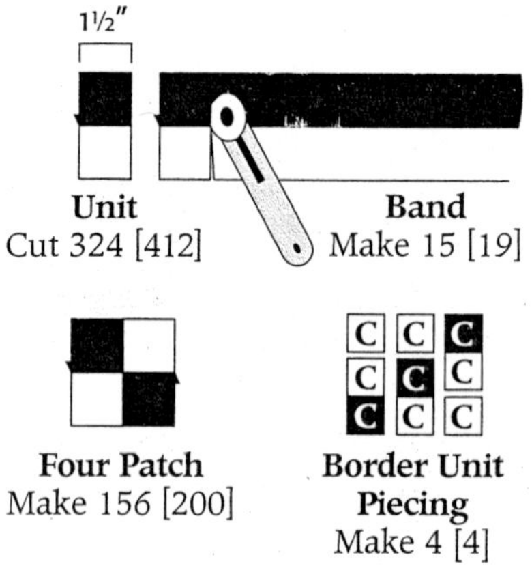

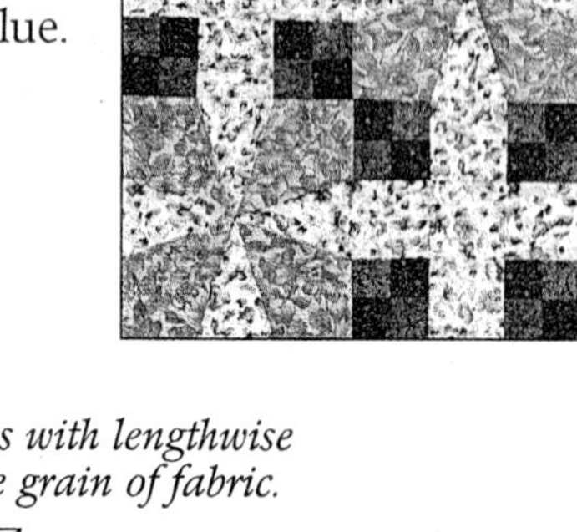

1½"

Unit
Cut 324 [412]

Band
Make 15 [19]

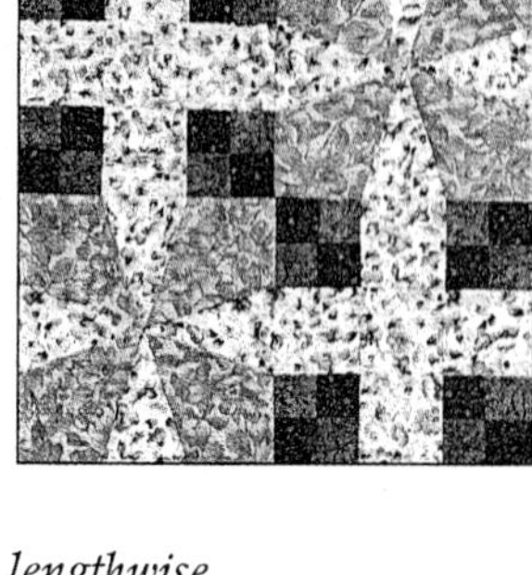

Four Patch
Make 156 [200]

Border Unit Piecing
Make 4 [4]

Triple Whammy

In each of these *Star Crossing* blocks, notice how the complement of the main color emphasizes one particular shape within the design.

Light green pinwheels spin against a red sky.

Little yellow squares dance across the quilt like twinkling stars.

Pale orange crosses form a grid on a background of blue.

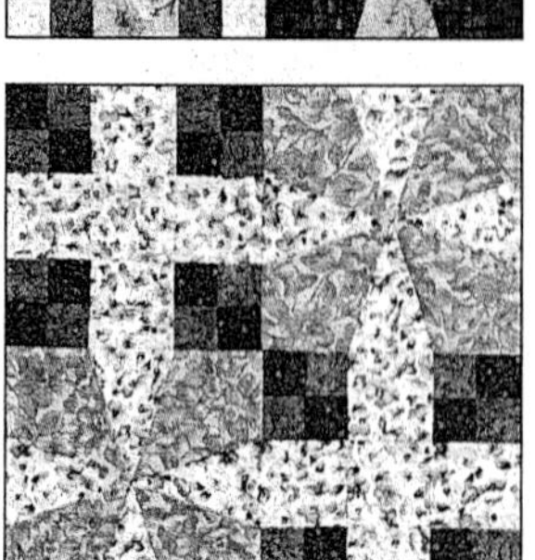

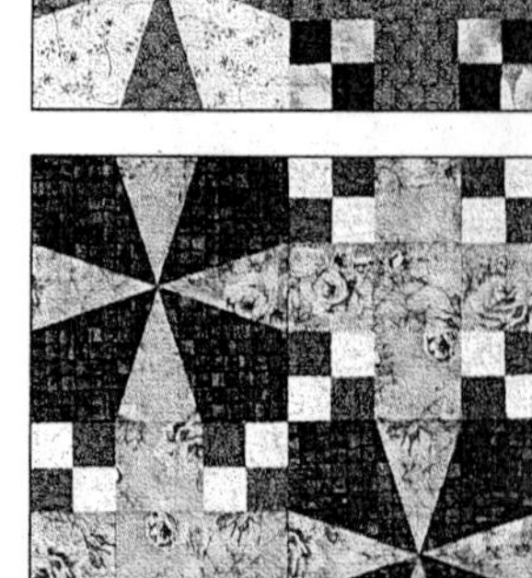

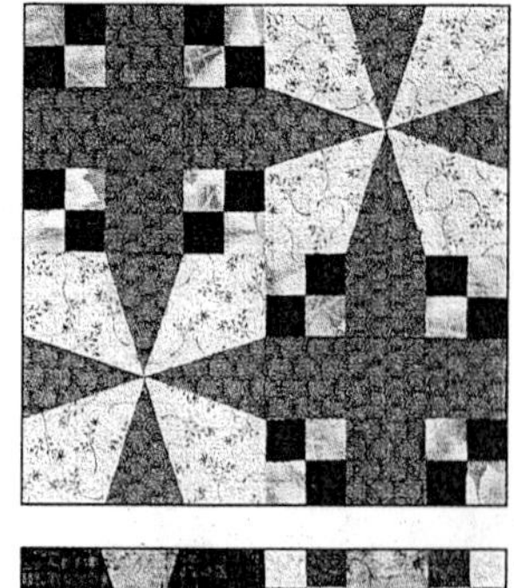

Trimming Template

Align arrows with lengthwise or crosswise grain of fabric.

For help using this template for patch A, see page 31.

Dimensions of diagramed patches include seam allowances.

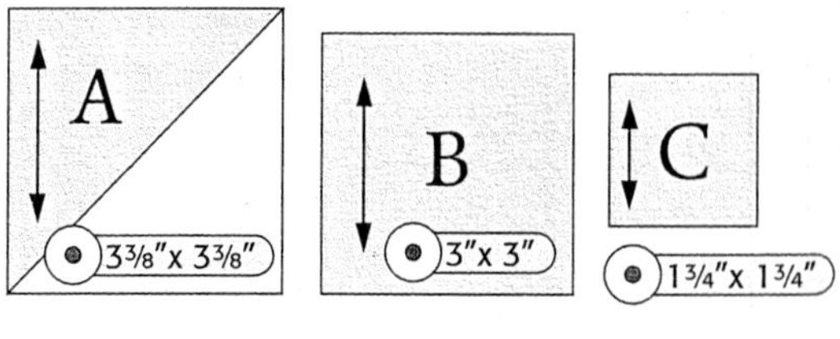

A
3⅜"x 3⅜"

B
3"x 3"

C
1¾"x 1¾"

SECOND SIGHT

BIENNIAL ❖ IV

SECOND SIGHT

BIENNIAL ∴ IV

Graham W. J. Beal

Foreword by Henry T. Hopkins

21 September–16 November 1986

San Francisco Museum of Modern Art

This book is published on the occasion of the exhibition SECOND SIGHT: BIENNIAL IV, organized by the San Francisco Museum of Modern Art and sponsored by the Museum's COLLECTORS FORUM. This exhibition has also been made possible by generous grants from the WELLS FARGO FOUNDATION and the National Endowment for the Arts. Additional support for the catalogue is provided by Charles Schwab & Co., Inc.

Collectors Forum gives additional thanks to the following generous contributors to the 1986 Biennial: GTE Sprint Communications Corporation; Inn at Union Square; Neiman Marcus and staff artist Allen Shaffer; Mrs. George Quist; Spectrum Foods; The Gap, Inc.; The Juliana Hotel; and Transamerica Corporation.

The San Francisco Museum of Modern Art is a member-supported, privately funded museum receiving major grants from the California Arts Council, the Institute of Museum Services, the James Irvine Foundation, the National Endowment for the Arts, the San Francisco Foundation, and the San Francisco Hotel Tax Fund.

Editing and Design: Ed Marquand Book Design
Composition: The Type Gallery, Seattle
Printing: Nissha Printing Co., Ltd., Kyoto

Cover:
Guilio Paolini
Nesso (Nessus), *1977 (detail)*
cat. no. 36

Library of Congress Cataloging-in-Publication Data
Beal, Graham William John.
Second sight.
Bibliography: p.
1. Art, Modern—20th century—Themes, motives—Exhibitions. 2. Avant-garde (Aesthetics)—History—20th century—Themes, motives—Exhibitions. I. San Francisco Museum of Modern Art. II. Title.
N6487.S2S253 1986 704.9'499 86-17839
ISBN 0-918471-08-7

Printed in Japan

Contents

Foreword

When graham beal accepted the position of Chief Curator at the San Francisco Museum of Modern Art, the first exhibition proposed for his origination was the fourth Biennial, sponsored by Collectors Forum, a major support group of the Museum. He suggested an exhibition of works by artists who draw on the art of the past to express humanist issues and ideals, a theme that received the unanimous support of the staff and the Collectors Forum advisory board. This catalogue documents the exhibition, *Second Sight: Biennial IV*.

Since the first Biennial six years ago, the format has gone through a series of significant changes that have helped to establish the program as unique. The first two exhibitions were national in scope, while the two most recent Biennials have become international, reflecting the wider geographical and cultural base of contemporary creative thought. The first two Biennials represented a diversity of visual expression. The last two have used binding themes (*The Human Condition, Second Sight*) to pinpoint areas of philosophical, historical, and aesthetic interest that cut across national boundaries and to which a number of contemporary artists adhere. It is important to note that while *Second Sight* looks at the contemporary influence of traditional themes, it is not an exhibition of art about art.

The San Francisco Museum of Modern Art Biennial continues to emphasize a limited number of artists, in this case nineteen, showing several works by each. And all four exhibitions have made a significant effort to present artists who are influencing the art world, but who have not been seen in depth in Bay Area museums.

I wish to thank the members of Collectors Forum for their continued commitment to this program as well as Graham Beal who, ably supported by Michael Schwager, Curatorial Assistant, organized the show. They join me in expressing their thanks to all the other staff involved in this exhibition—most notably Pam Pack, Associate Registrar; Kent Roberts and the installation crew; Kathleen Ferres, Curatorial Secretary; Marcia Tanner, Director of Public Relations; Jo Rowlings, Public Relations Assistant; Kathleen Rydar, Director of Development; Robert Whyte, Director of Education; and Beau Takahara, Interpretive Programs Assistant. I also wish to thank the many artists, museums, collectors, and dealers who have lent valuable works to this exhibition.

Henry T. Hopkins
Director

Collectors Forum Foreword

THE COLLECTORS FORUM is proud to present the fourth biennial exhibition of the San Francisco Museum of Modern Art, *Second Sight: Biennial IV*. We are particularly pleased as this year's Biennial represents the inaugural exhibition curated by Graham Beal.

Second Sight is the first museum exhibition to focus solely on the phenomenon of American and European sculptors and painters who, departing dramatically from post-World War II modernist styles, are incorporating the rich imagery and techniques of older art traditions into their own unmistakably contemporary art. This Biennial is in keeping with Collectors Forum's tradition of sponsoring major exhibitions on current, important themes in international art.

Collectors Forum, a support organization of the Museum, is composed of collectors who not only donate major funding for the Biennial, but also, through the Biennial Committee, work closely with the staff to organize and coordinate funding, publicity, opening events, and the Symposium. This year, Gardiner Hempel and Chotsie Blank, as cochairmen, their committees, and the museum staff have done an extraordinary job and have our deepest gratitude. Oni Berglund, the Collectors Forum coordinator, also deserves special mention for her enormous help during the past year.

And finally, I would like to take this opportunity to specially recognize Henry Hopkins, the Museum's Director, who has guided Collectors Forum through the years and has been so instrumental in our success. His knowledge, humor, and style have given us a deeper appreciation for the art and the Museum that we all care about so much.

Anne MacDonald Walker
Collectors Forum President, 1986

Lenders to the Exhibition

Private and Corporate Lenders

Siah Armajani
John and Marcia Bachner
BankAmerica Corporation Art Collection
John Berggruen
Robert and Maryse Boxer
Edward R. Downe, Jr.
Agnes Gund
Anne and William J. Hokin Collection
Byron Meyer
PaineWebber Group Inc. Collection
Mr. and Mrs. Richard F. Polich
Donald J. Putterman and Adrienne Sherman
Wilhelm Shurman
Mr. and Mrs. Jerome Siegel
Mr. and Mrs. Sidney Singer
Martin Sklar
Mrs. Earl Staley
M. Louise Stanley
Pat Steir
Michelle Stuart

Museums and Galleries

Rena Bransten Gallery, San Francisco
Diane Brown Gallery, New York
Ronald Feldman Fine Arts Inc., New York
Marian Goodman Gallery, New York
Martina Hamilton Gallery, New York
Jane Haslem Gallery, Washington, D.C.
Hirshhorn Museum and Sculpture Garden,
Smithsonian Institution, Washington, D.C.
Phyllis Kind Gallery, New York
Michael Klein, Inc., New York
Richard Kuhlenschmidt Gallery, Los Angeles
Metropolitan Museum of Art, New York
Max Protetch Gallery, New York
San Francisco Museum of Modern Art
Sander Gallery, New York
Ruth Siegel Ltd, New York
Sperone Westwater, New York
Texas Gallery, Houston
Bruce Velick Gallery, San Francisco
Virginia Museum of Fine Arts, Richmond
Whitney Museum of American Art, New York

A Little History

IT IS FROM ITALY that we launch through the world this violently upsetting, incendiary manifesto of ours. With it, today, we establish <u>Futurism</u> because we want to free this land from its smelly gangrene of professors, archaeologists, ciceroni, and antiquarians. For too long has Italy been a dealer in secondhand clothes. We mean to free her from the numberless museums that cover her like so many graveyards.

Museums; cemeteries! . . . Identical, surely, in the sinister promiscuity of so many bodies unknown to one another. Museums: public dormitories where one lies forever beside hated or unknown beings. Museums: absurd abattoirs of painters and sculptors ferociously macerating each other with color-blows and line-blows, the length of the fought-over walls! . . .

And what is there to see in an old picture except the laborious contortions of an artist throwing himself against the barriers that thwart his desire to express his dream completely? Admiring an old picture is the same as pouring our sensibility into a funerary urn instead of hurling it far off, in violent spasms of action and creation.

Do you, then, wish to waste all your best powers in this eternal and futile workship of the past, from which you emerge fatally exhausted, shrunken, beaten down?

In truth I tell you that daily visits to museums, libraries, and academies (cemeteries of empty exertion, calvaries of crucified dreams, registries of aborted beginnings!) is, for artists, as damaging as the prolonged supervision by parents of certain young people drunk with their talent and their ambitious wills. When the future is barred to them, the admirable past may be a solace for the ills of the moribund, the sickly, the prisoner. . . . But we want no part of it, the past, we the young and strong <u>Futurists!</u> . . .

So let them come, the [blithe] incendiaries with charred fingers! Here they are! Here they are! . . . Come on! set fire to the library shelves! Turn aside the canals to flood the museums! . . . Oh, the joy of seeing the glorious old canvases bobbing adrift on those waters, discolored and shredded! . . . Take up your pickaxes, your axes and hammers, and wreck, wreck the venerable cities, pitilessly![1]

THUS, IN HIS 1909 manifesto, did the Italian futurist poet Marinetti identify the art of the past as the twentieth-century artist's "public enemy number one." He was not alone, and though his political views were subsequently to distance him from his fellow-travelers, his violent idealism was shared by the partisans of modernism across Europe. From Guillaume Apollinaire and Robert Delaunay in Paris to Natalia Goncharova and Mikhail Larionov in Moscow, from Franz Marc and Wassily Kandinsky in Munich to Percy Wyndam Lewis and Jacob Epstein in London, whatever their differences (and there were many), they shared the idea of the artist as a revolutionary figure in opposition to a complacent and unimaginative society. To one degree or another these artists saw themselves as part of a much wider movement that sought to change the world and to build a modern society through purely modern means. Everything was to be rethought, reordered, and reinvented. To borrow from Wyndam Lewis's facetious definition of futurism, truly twentieth-century art must address ". . . the Present with the Past rigidly excluded."2

New truths required new forms. The urgently felt need for an uncontaminated language expressly invented for the twentieth century led to a heavy emphasis on style, and for the first three-quarters of this century, movement and style were virtually synonymous. With several notable exceptions, every movement was given a title that ended with "ism": cubism, orphism, purism, surrealism, expressionism, to mention just a few. One of the exceptions to this rule was the Dutch movement De Stijl (the title simply translates as "the Style"), whose content has been summed up as ". . . harmony that . . . can only be rendered by abstract means, through compositions unhampered by associations with objects in the external world. This search for harmony was the springboard and constant goal of De Stijl. Yet De Stijl artists were not solely concerned with aesthetics. The movement was an effort to renew the links between life and art. In creating a new visual style it attempted to create a new style for living."3 In De Stijl, then, as was the case with so much European modernism, formal innovation was seen as an expression of a basically utopian goal. Artists felt themselves to be workers in the aesthetic quarries, shaping the visual blocks from which the new society was to be built. Looking back on the 1930s Barbara Hepworth summed it up: "Everywhere there seemed to be abundant energy, and a developing interest in fusion of all the arts to some great purpose."4 Such aspirations were cruelly disappointed when, in that same decade, reaction replaced revolution. In Italy, Germany, and Russia, idealist artists were surprised to find themselves discredited (or worse) by the new political leaders. In the reactionary suppression that followed revolutionary efforts, the integrity of international modernism was shattered. With World War II its momentum was violently stopped.

When the modernist phoenix rose, to most people's surprise, it did so in New York and in a significantly mutated form. As one not entirely approving critic wrote: "The French fathered the Modern Movement, which slowly moved beyond the channel and then across the Irish Sea until the Americans finally took it over, bringing to it their own demonic energy, extremism and taste for the colossal."5 Though specifically written about literature, those last words—"demonic energy," "extremism," "colossal"—are not a bad starting point for a working definition of abstract expressionism, the movement that shifted the center of modernist gravity from Paris to New York. European artists—at least the younger ones—had little doubt that in the work of Pollock, de Kooning, and others they were confronting a new order of painting characterized by "size, energy, originality, economy and inventive daring . . . [whose] creative emptiness represented a radical discovery . . . as did their flatness, or rather their spatial shallowness. . . ."6

One of the consequences of modernism's migration to America was the loss of its sociopolitical pretensions; art became, first and foremost, a matter of individual expression. This is not to say that American painting was apolitical. Robert Motherwell's *Spanish Elegy* paintings, for example, are eloquent denunciations of repression in Franco's Spain, but such political content is personal and commentative in nature. The

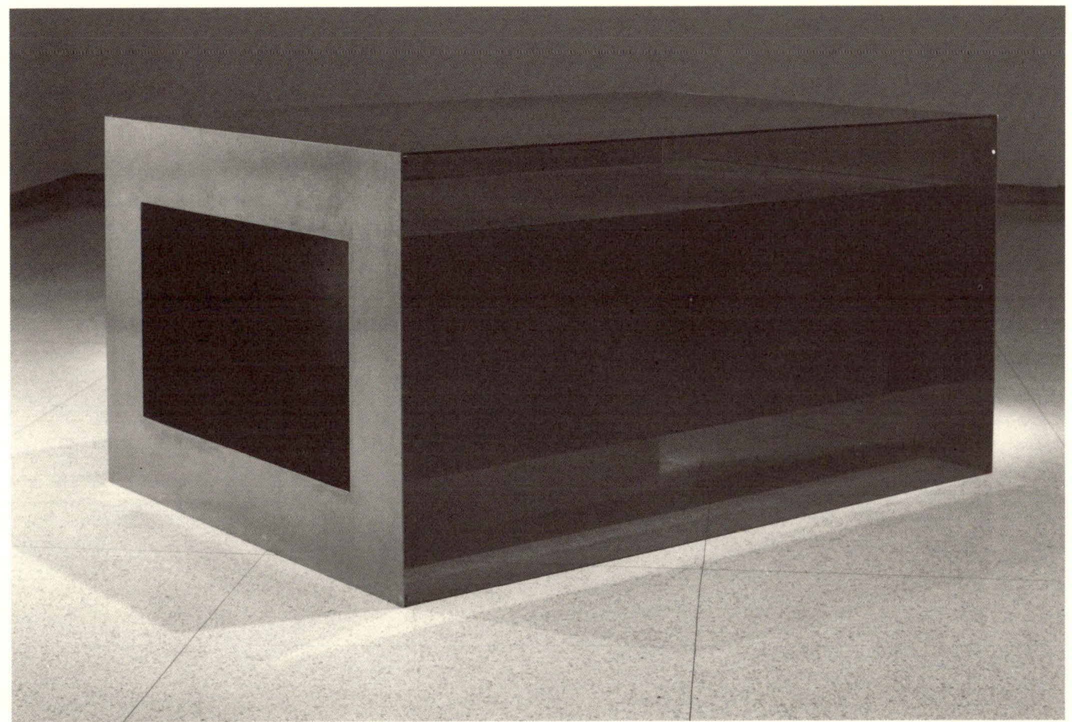

Figure 1. Donald Judd, *Untitled*, 1968, stainless steel, blue plexiglas, 33 x 68 x 48″, Walker Art Center, Minneapolis.

paintings are not, save in the most general sense, part of an attempt to build a new world in the context of an old one. Rather the opposite: artists in America in the immediate post-war period rejoiced at the absence of an identifiable cultural context, particularly at the lack of the dead weight of history. As Barnett Newman asserted, giving the modernist antihistorical bias a new twist:

> We are freeing ourselves of the impediments of memory, association, nostalgia, legend, myth, or what have you, that have been the devices of western European painting. Instead of making *cathedrals* out of Christ, man, or "life," we are making it out of ourselves, out of our own feelings. The image we produce is the self-evident one of revelation, real and concrete, that can be understood by anyone who will look at it without the nostalgic glasses of history.[7]

Thus revolution was perceived to have been replaced by revelation; the old world was no longer an impediment, it was simply irrelevant. The "Brave New World" was, it seemed, now to be built on a brand new frontier.

Crisis, however, was not far away. Within a few years artists were addressing the issue of what kind of life existed for them beyond abstract expressionism. The vitality of much work produced in the 1950s tended to obscure the fact that the critical debate underlying modernism was being significantly narrowed and focused increasingly on the means of expression. More and more, the business of art became art, and while much of the demanding painting and sculpture of the 1960s—that of, say, Frank Stella and Sol

LeWitt—drew strength from its rigorous testing of the means of each discipline, modernism's formalist urge to define the essentials of visual art devolved in its later manifestations into a multiplicity of stylistic options, each one deriving justification for its existence as a "logical" response to a previous movement. The minimalist cube (fig. 1), in all its reticent elegance, perfectly symbolizes the end of the modernist debate. On the one hand it sums up the multidisciplinary aspirations of modernism: it is sculpture, but draws upon painting, architecture, and design. On the other, its relationship to issues outside gallery walls is, to say the least, tenuous, having removed itself to a domain where only sensory effect matters. As Charles Newman has remarked: "Liberation from history exacts its own boredom and determinism."8

The final step in this "logical" sequence was the actual disappearance of the object itself, which was replaced by information conveyed by language and photographic documentation. But, in that concept was now more important than execution, conceptual art was both the apotheosis of formalism and its nemesis. Through conceptualism formalist theories were unified with those of Marcel Duchamp, who, as early as 1917, had claimed to be "more interested in ideas than in the final product." Suddenly, in the years around 1970, intellectual activity elbowed optical response from the limelight of avant-garde art. In reasserting that anything could be art, conceptualism refocused attention on such things as content and personal meaning, elements hitherto regarded as antithetical to modernist practice.

Liberated by conceptualism and often impelled by awareness of social and political issues, artists of the 1970s used their work as vehicles for expressing non-art ideas with increasing aggressiveness. Feminism, autobiography, ecological issues, and much more became springboards for a revitalized, reoriented, and openly pluralist art that appropriated whatever was most convenient for the expression of its ideas. It is, therefore, hardly surprising that in this new atmosphere artists should avail themselves of the art of the past. It was not as if, on a personal level, they had ever ceased to look at it. Some had even openly referred to it, but with few exceptions, the modernist artists' appropriation of "old" art was laden with irony and tended to devalue it. Though Francis Bacon may wish his paintings of the pope to be seen in direct reference to the original Velásquez (and thereby enriched by it), artists of the 1960s who used well-known images from art history did so occasionally and, even then, very much within the framework of their own established stylistic practices.

To less established artists working in the late 1970s and 1980s, the art of the past offered more than a chance for a few stylistic pyrotechnics. These artists regard the creations of their forebears as aids to meaning, as a way of broadening their frames of reference. Giulio Paolini, who first attracted attention in the U.S. as an exponent of the conceptually based Italian movement Arte Povera, has more recently availed himself of his Italian heritage. His combinations of antique plaster casts, drawings on paper, and cloth are, he says, carefully calculated to give the viewer the feeling of being the "author of [the] work. . . . I know that a foundation, a repository of traditions, exists in our culture for the way we interpret the efficacy of a work of art, in short, for the way in which we communicate."9 So convinced of the specificity of this repository is Paolini that he sees his " . . . palette [as] consolidated in a tradition that is not Anglo-Saxon." Whatever the individual's cultural origins, Paolini relies upon the viewer to bring his or her preconceptions to the work. A plaster cast, such as the one used in *Nesso* (cat. no. 36), is not "a revisit, in the sense of a choice in the stores of the past, but rather an undifferentiated welcome, a memory that wants to reach the very making of the work."[10] Confronted by this elegant combination of startlingly disparate parts, the viewer is put on the spot. There is no question of how the work is constructed (a red silk scarf of extravagant proportions is wrapped around a scroll of paper inscribed with a head and torso atop a horse's body to constitute a centaur); the question is why. Paolini's resolute neutrality is perfectly calculated to propel the viewer, sooner rather than later, towards this implacable query. "I would like," he concludes, "to restore all the intense activity and labor of past works, all the flavor of the museum. I have no preference for style, I am attracted to *why* anyone makes art."[11]

Paolini, nevertheless, makes good use of his Mediterranean heritage. *Nesso* is an economical combination of the main actors in the episode that ultimately led to the death of the Greek hero Hercules. Nessus, so the story goes, was a centaur ferryman. While carrying the hero's wife, Deianira, across a river he attempted to ravish her, but was slain by Hercules. Later Nessus's blood became a fatal potion that, rubbed into the hero's raiment by Deianira, was to be the instrument of Hercules' death. The human part of *Nesso* is, in fact, a line drawing based on a Hellenistic statue of Hercules, while the silk scarf can be taken to represent both blood and Deianira, who in some ancient renderings is depicted on the back of Nessus, her robes streaming in the winds. Paolini cannot be sure that, today, a viewer—even one from his own culture—will be familiar with the specifics of this tale of passion and death. Any interpretation will tend to be personal and unpredictable, a variable by-product of a process calculated to question the urge to create.

Given its long-standing disrepute in the eyes of the avant-garde, the use of classical antiquity as a shock tactic is doubly effective. Its partial resuscitation in the 1920s, by Picasso and others, was completely overshadowed by its more straightforward but far less salutary appropriation by the emerging dictators of the period, and since then, references in modern art to classical culture have, on the whole, been tentative, limited largely to the evocative use of mythological names as titles for individual works of art.

The notion that old stories can yield new meanings by being retold underlies many of Stephen McKenna's paintings. His precise approach to a myth varies from painting to painting, from the bland fresco style of *Europe* (cat. no. 30) to the imitation sarcophagus relief of *Destruction of Acteon* (cat. no. 32) and the old master look-alike of *The Blind Orion with Eos and Artemis* (cat. no. 31). This last picture is closely based on a work by the seventeenth-century classicist Nicolas Poussin (fig. 2), a man whom McKenna admires as:

> . . . a great moral idealist but able to embody his morality in the most tender of expressions. . . . Born without any great facility, in an age of virtuosi like Rubens and Bernini, he slowly and patiently developed a pictorial language capable of sustaining the breadth and grandeur of his concerns. . . . For the spectator, Poussin's stories provide both information and the stimulus to acquire more.[12]

The story of Orion is long and complex, but the modern viewer can work out much from the painting. The blinded giant is being led toward the healing light; in his path stands Artemis, who, though initially helpful to Orion, will accidentally be responsible for his death. Though faithful to the original Poussin in overall conception, McKenna's handling of paint owes much to Magritte (a similarity that is heightened by strange juxtapositions of day and night and unexpected shifts of scale), and unlike old master paintings, McKenna's canvases do not really attempt to fool the eye. It is, in fact, important to

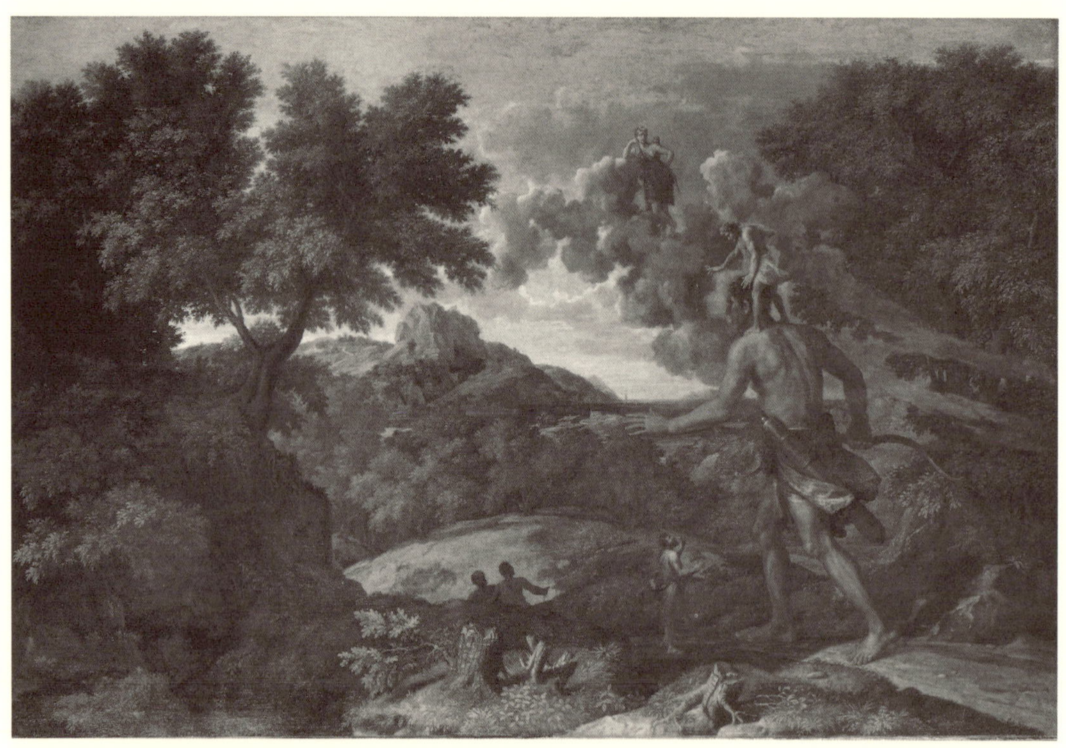

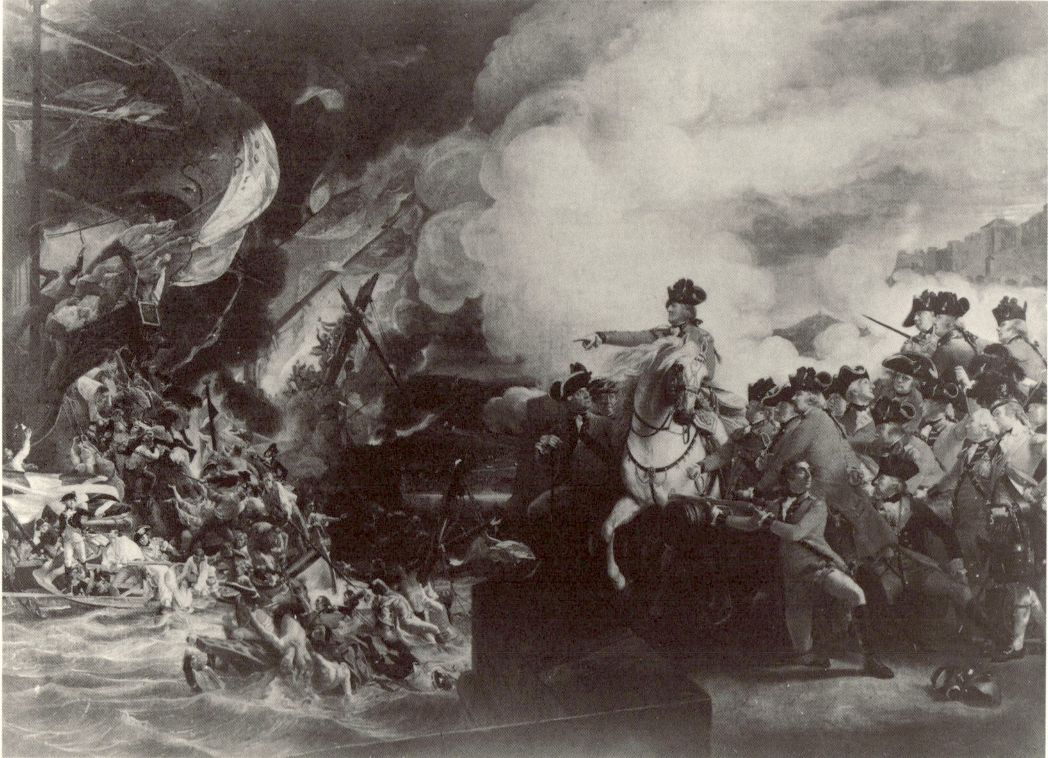

ABOVE: Figure 2. Nicholas Poussin, *The Blind Orion Searching for the Rising Sun*, 1638, oil on canvas, 46⅞ x 72″, The Metropolitan Museum of Art, Fletcher Fund, New York. BELOW: Figure 3. John Singleton Copley, *The Siege and Relief of Gibraltar, 13 September 1782*, c. 1783, 53 x 74¾″, The Tate Gallery, London.

this artist that the viewer be fully aware of his convention and decisions, for in this way attention is quickly returned to the story.

Proponents of classicism argue that the limitations of its rules, be it the well-known myth or architectural orders, actually serve to highlight individual contributions of particular artists, and even at a time when classical learning is all but defunct, references to such things as the Acropolis are hardly likely to go astray. In *Galvanized Temple* (cat. no. 10), Roger Brown wittily uses garbage cans to produce a dumpy version of the building type that symbolizes a wide range of phenomena, from pagan spirituality to nineteenth-century banking. The shaped sides of Brown's cans echo the fluted forms of classical columns, just as the mottled sparkle of the metal evokes the glitter of polished marble. For Brown, who has long been a practitioner of narrative painting, *Galvanized Temple* represents an unusual excursion into classicism and into sculpture, but like much of his work, this modestly sized object is a comment on the loss of innocence that comes with failed dreams. Heaven and the gutter, the work suggests, are not so far apart. The theme of loss of innocence is also found in his acerbic *Giotto and Chicago,* a reworking of the great Florentine painter's fresco cycle in Padua to tell the story of art and criticism in contemporary Chicago. The theme is, of course, directly addressed in his 1982 painting *Adam and Eve (Expulsion from the Garden)* (cat. no. 9), Brown's reworking of the oldest story with just the slightest nod toward Masaccio.

The light of reason so commonly associated with antiquity is left far behind in the work of Ann McCoy. Her meticulous drawings and sculpture explore a nocturnal world of dreams and death in which animal and human forms intermingle and conjoin among religious monuments and artifacts. A follower of psychologist C. G. Jung, McCoy sees the rejection of the "dark pagan side of the psyche" as not just dangerous but directly self-destructive. "With all our 'rationality,'." she has written,

> . . . we have forgotten an essential psychic fact, that our society is a thin veneer over a still pagan structure. The events of Germany in the '30s and '40s are a warning to us that overemphasis of the "rational" at the expense of the transformation of the inner pagan opens the gates of hell and destruction.[13]

As her statement in this catalogue makes clear, each of McCoy's works illustrates a carefully thought-out program with an avowed moral purpose, and similar aims can be seen in Louise Stanley's inversions of Greek myths.

A certain moral tone underlies the nearly abstract canvases of Christopher Le Brun. Much of his earlier imagery derived from the landscape paintings of Claude Lorraine and Nicolas Poussin, but his more recent work draws more upon such proponents of moral and historical painting as John Singleton Copley (fig. 3) or Benjamin West. Stripped of specifics of time and place, Le Brun's proud horses invariably symbolize the spirit of hope, adventure, and even victory. But just as the white horse symbolizes these beneficial qualities, other colors in his canvases stand for the adversity against which the spirit must struggle.

In the eminently legible paintings of Carlo Maria Mariani art turns in on itself. In *La Mano Ubbidisce all'Intelletto (The Hand Submits to the Intellect)* (cat. no. 23), two figures crowned with the laurel wreathes of victory are seated, one on a cube, the other on a sphere. The figures can be read both as humans indulging in a little antique body art, or they can alternately be read as painter and painted image. Mariani's sleight of hand momentarily obscures the fact that they are both painted images. The picture addresses the narcissicism inherent in much self-expression, and the figures are disturbing for the sense of stupefaction that seems to result from their artistic activities.

Mariani's ambivalence toward the figure and the act of expression is not shared by Odd Nerdrum, who dares to paint in a manner recalling Rembrandt and Gericault. Nerdrum returns to old-fashioned figurative painting as if it were the only appropriate vehicle for dealing adequately with the ultimate questions of mankind's survival. In Nerdrum's world the past, present, and future are combined to depict scenes in which the precariousness of continued existence is frankly addressed. In *Iron Law* (cat. no. 33) the story of Cain and Abel (man's first inhumanity to man) is retold as the identifiable and endlessly repeated source of our woes. In a passage that (unexpectedly perhaps) links Nerdrum to McCoy, Donald Kuspit has commented:

> Nerdrum is, in my opinion, a religious painter. . . . It has been argued that the success of modernity is that it has been able to transcend the tragic sense of life through the scientific mastery of nature . . . the failure of modernity is that it ignores, or attempts to sidestep, the tragic issue of death—and the issue of tragic death. [14]

To some artists, the failure of the old modernist cause offered the opportunity to examine all means of visual expression, and Komar and Melamid, trained as social realists in the Soviet Union, use their academic skills to question the ability of any single style to tell universal truths. In *Venus of Milo* (cat. no. 19) a dead era's epitome of expressive power is resuscitated by the addition of graffiti arms wielding hammer and sickle; classical Europe, revolutionary Russia, and pop-culture New York are brought together to create an image with the power to amuse and alarm. In other works, such as *Nostalgic View of the Kremlin from Manhattan* (cat. no. 18), they have explored the ability of art actively to mislead, and most recently, by juxtaposing panels painted with different images and techniques, they emphasize the infinite number of options open to the artist today.

Pat Steir also examines options and means. In the 1970s her work revolved around basic marks—dashes, dots, diagonal crosses—and a few emblematic images, notably flowers. Recent work has concentrated on a group of themes strongly associated with particular artists: the flowers of Jan Breughel and Vincent van Gogh, the waves of Gustav Courbet, Leonardo da Vinci, and Hokusai. These paintings, usually consisting of three or more panels, are about the choices an artist makes in depicting a subject in a certain way and about the limitations as well as the scope that inevitably accompany subjective expression. But Steir's work is not purely serial, nor is it analytical in any pseudoscientific way; the overall effect of her visual catalogues and combinations is one of ebullience and assertion, echoing her sense of wonder at the myriad ways of depicting the same motif.

Mark Tansey turns the tables on all commentators and codifiers in his elaborate misreading of art historical and critical terminology. The descriptive title of his painting *Triumph of the New York School* (cat. no. 51) refers to a well-known textbook, *The Triumph of American Painting* by Irving Sandler. In Tansey's painting the hegemonic phraseology of much art writing is taken at face value, and the French army is depicted surrendering to their U.S. counterparts. One of the senior French officers looks very like Pablo Picasso; others resemble Guillaume Apollinaire, Marcel Duchamp, and Fernand Léger. In the American ranks can be spotted the features of Jackson Pollock, Clement Greenberg,

Barnett Newman, David Smith, and others. The more technically advanced U.S. troops have tanks and armored cars, while the outdated French have cavalry. The overall composition of *Triumph of the New York School* is close to Diego Velásquez's *Surrender of Breda* of 1634, a depiction of an act of chivalry in the otherwise unforgiving Thirty Years War. *Surrender at Breda* is, in a sense, a glorification of war through art; *Triumph of the New York School* uses war to glorify art. In the landscape background, itself a cross between Velásquez's battlefield and Bosch's scenes of hell, little figures can be seen in a state of torment. One man beats his head against a wall (a quotation from another Tansey painting, *Short History of Modern Painting*) in much the same way that American painters in the 1960s tormented themselves with the doctrine of two-dimensionality.

Tansey combines the scale of traditional history painting with the appearance of news photographs, and much of his work assumes the position of reportage. *The Innocent Eye Test* (cat. no. 49) depicts the unveiling of a painting to a very special judge. The painting is Paulus Potter's *Young Bull* of 1647, now in the Mauritshuis, a picture once regarded as the epitome of realism and described by a nineteenth-century critic as being "as near perfection as the art will ever attain."[15] In Tansey's picture, this notion is severely tested. The judge is a cow. What better way to assess the perfection of a picture of a bull than to bring in a judge who has no preconceived notions about art, but who has, presumably, a very strong sense of what constitutes cowness. Around her, experts look on deferentially; one stands by with a mop in the event of some critical indiscretion on the part of the judge.

But Tansey's real target is usually twentieth-century criticism, and in *The Innocent Eye Test* he focuses on two contradictory strands of late modernist thought: one, that art, being "purely optical," can be understood instantaneously, without any other reference points; the other, the tendency to subject art to pseudoscientific methodologies. So, the cow looks dumbly at the painting and a white-coated technician makes notes. Such attitudes left to themselves, Tansey feels, break down conventions to the point of meaninglessness. They leave no room for the complexity of perception, and in particular, they fail to account for the great wealth of experience and references that each individual brings to bear when looking at a work of art. How, Tansey asks, do we see things, and how do we establish that they are true?

Siah Armajani's attitudes represent both a throwback to early modernist social ideals and a refutation of late modernism's aesthetic practices of segregating the artistic disciplines from one another, and from the rest of culture. Reflecting the philosophies of a wide range of democrats, radicals, and visionaries, Armajani's works are a plea for cultural and self-awareness. Thomas Jefferson, Thomas Paine, Walt Whitman, Frank Lloyd Wright, and El Lissitsky are just a few of the individuals whose ideals are given expression in complex sculptures that combine architectural and utilitarian forms. In his *Dictionary for Building* series Armajani explores basic architectural features common to domestic building; each sculpture is a definition and an elaboration. *Hall Mirror with Table in Front* (fig. 4) bears, in gilded capitals, philosopher John Dewey's epithet: "As long as art is the beauty parlor of civilization, neither art nor civilization is secure." By asking viewers to examine forms in the context of their own day-to-day behavior, Armajani literally gives meaning to space.

Lost cultures and distant lands are the subjects of Michelle Stuart's wall pieces. The patterns of her 1982 *Nazca Lines Star Chart* (fig. 5) are from the ancient and mysterious Peruvian monument. Embedded in the gridlike field of "tiles" of earth-impregnated

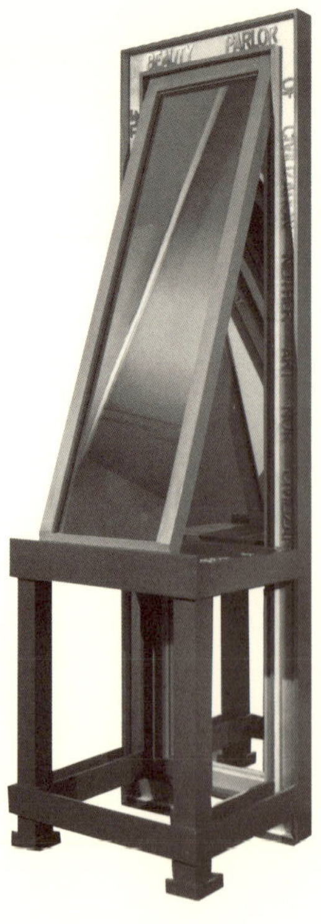

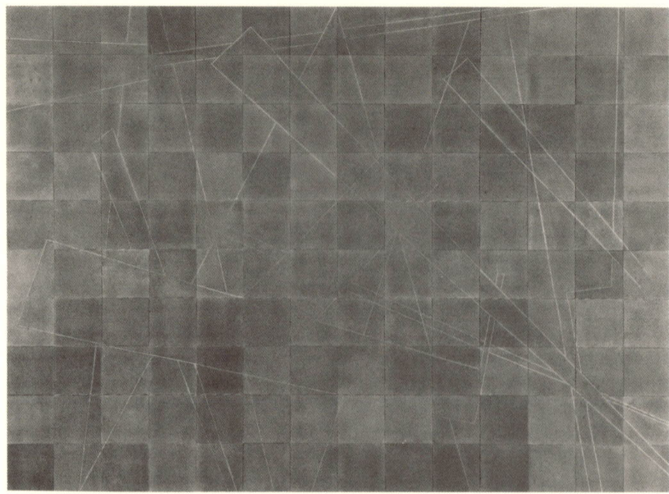

LEFT: Figure 4. Siah Armajani, *Dictionary for Building: Hall Mirror with Table in Front*, 1983-84, bronze, mirror, painted wood, 84 x 24 ¼ x 26 ¼", Courtesy Max Protetch Gallery, New York. ABOVE: Figure 5. Michelle Stuart, *Nazca Lines Star Chart*, 1981-82, earth from Nazca, Peru, on paper, 120 x 168", The Museum of Modern Art, New York, gift of William S. Paley.

paper, the lines initially seem random. The artist claims that they are, most likely, astronomical aids. Thus earth and sky are figuratively combined in a work that literally fuses aesthetic, scientific, and geological elements. Recently Stuart has moved away from the specificity of *Nazca Lines Star Chart*. In *Red . . . Earth. Dream Wall of the Bighouse* (cat. no. 48), archaeological and geological fragments float in a dense earth-red field—shadowy elements that evoke precious life long disappeared. Drawing attention to these fragile echoes of vanished activity, Stuart emphasizes mankind's history as one long, continuous experiment in culture. Stuart's work, while possessing the poetic force of much of the best of post-war American painting, concerns itself with such broader and increasingly urgent issues as ecology and survival. As is the case with a number of artists in this exhibition, Stuart's use of the art of the past is intended to make the viewer not just more responsive to the visual world, but more responsible in the real one.

THE IDEA THAT art has a broader moral purpose is certainly not new. In the nineteenth century it was explicitly and beautifully stated by John Ruskin, and it is implicit in much of the artistic endeavor of the twentieth century. The forceful reemergence of humanist issues in art is both remarkable and, to this writer at least, laudable. Notions that the strenuous and high-minded efforts of younger artists represent " . . . a betrayal of the high purposes and moral grandeur of Modernism in its heyday" are, to say the least, surprising.[17] If the achievements of Pablo Picasso or Jackson Pollock have any lasting value—and surely they do—they will withstand any realignments of taste that such critics find so antipathetic to the "imperatives of Modernism," just as Michelangelo and Bronzino's work survived the Council of Trent and fed into the sensibility now known as the baroque. In writing about artists who employ the "unmodernist" tactic of drawing

10

upon the art of the past, I have avoided the term postmodern; partly because it is used so loosely, but mainly because so much of their work is clearly based on modernist achievements.

In its revolutionary, formative years, modernism rejected out of hand previous artistic achievements as bourgeois and useless. The early results were promising and their application was widespread. By the 1960s modernism found itself assimilated and institutionalized, its proponents indulging in dialogues of little concern to anyone outside their own circles (whose numbers were, admittedly, swelled by the art boom of the last couple of decades). In seriously challenging the hermeticism of much late modernism there has been a "redefinition of the role of art and artists." [18] Artists have been seeking ways to make their work convey more than a handful of aesthetic notions, and part of this effort has been a measured reevaluation of the art of the past. Not for the sake of some sort of latter-day scholastic discourse, nor to flaunt "discoveries made among the ruins as . . . models of excellence and guides to creation." [19] Rather, these artists draw selectively on the art of the past, seeking neither role models nor plunder but revitalized and flexible modes of expression capable of asking serious questions and giving compelling form to strongly felt ideals.

Notes

1. F. T. Marinetti, "The Founding and Manifesto of Futurism," *Le Figaro* (Paris) February 20, 1909, in *Marinetti: Selected Writings*, trans. R. W. Flint, (New York: Farrar, Strauss and Giroux, 1972), pp. 42-43.

2. Percy Wyndam Lewis, foreword to *Exhibition of English Post-Impressionists, Cubists and Others*, 1913, in *Wyndam Lewis on Art*, ed. W. Michel and C. J. Fox, (New York, 1969), p. 56.

3. H. L. C. Jaffe, introduction to *De Stijl: 1917–1931, Visions of Utopia*, ed. Mildred Friedman, (Minneapolis: Walker Art Center; New York: Abbeville, 1982), p. 11.

4. B. Hepworth, *Barbara Hepworth: Carvings and Drawings*, (London: Lund Humphries, 1952), n. pag.

5. C. Connolly, *The Modern Movement: One Hundred Key Books from England, France and America, 1880–1950* (London: A. Deutsch, 1965), p. 4.

6. P. Heron, review of "Americans at the Tate Gallery," *Arts*, March 1956, p. 17.

7. B. Newman, "The Ides of Art, Six Opinions on What is Sublime Art?" *Tigers Eye*, December 1948, p. 53. Newman's sentiments are, however, strikingly in the tradition of the Hudson River School of landscape painting, whose founder, Thomas Cole, had written: "You see no ruined tower to tell of outrage, no gorgeous temple to speak of ostentation, but freedom's offspring — peace, security, and happiness dwell there, the spirits of the scene . . . . And in looking over the yet uncultured scene, the mind's eye may see far into futurity." "Essay on American Scenery," 1835, in *American Art 1700–1900, Sources and Documents*, ed. John W. McCoubrey, (Englewood Cliffs, New Jersey: Prentice-Hall, 1965), p. 108.

8. C. Newman, *The Post-Modern Aura: The Act of Fiction in an Age of Inflation*, (Evanston: Northwestern University Press, 1985), p. 39.

9. J. Taylor, "A Conversation with Giulio Paolini," *The Print Collectors Newsletter*, (Nov–Dec 1984), p. 166.

10. Artist's statement, 1983, in *Giulio Paolini Intentions/Figures*, vol. 1, (Lyons: Le Nouveau Musee, 1984), p. 85. *English Text*, trans. Isabelle Lenoir, p. 11.

11. Ibid.

12. "Extracts from a Conversation between Barry Barker and Stephen McKenna in Brussels, February, 1981," in *Stephen McKenna: Subjects, Scenes and Stories*, (Belfast: Arts Council of Northern Ireland, 1981), n. pag.

13. A. McCoy, "Meditation on the Red Mass," *Bomb*, Winter 1986, no. 15, p. 38.

14. D. Kuspit, "Odd Nerdrum: The Human Constant," in *Odd Nerdrum, Recent Paintings* (New York: Martina Hamilton Gallery and Germans Van Eck Gallery, 1986).

15. J. Smith, *A Catalogue Raisonne of the Most Eminent Dutch, Flemish and French Painters*, (London 1829–42).

16. H. Kramer, "Postmodern: art and culture in the 1980s," *The New Criterion*, I, 1982, p. 42.

17. Ibid, p. 37.

18. H. Fox, "The Will to Meaning," in *Content: A Contemporary Focus*, (Washington, D. C.: Hirshborn Museum and Sculpture Garden, 1984), p. 23.

19. Kramer, op cit.

Artists in the Exhibition

Hermann Albert

Edward Allington

Siah Armajani

Roger Brown

Harry Fritzius

Douglas Higgins

David Hollowell

Komar and Melamid

Christopher Le Brun

Carlo Maria Mariani

Ann McCoy

Stephen McKenna

Odd Nerdrum

Giulio Paolini

Earl Staley

M. Louise Stanley

Pat Steir

Michelle Stuart

Mark Tansey

Hermann Albert

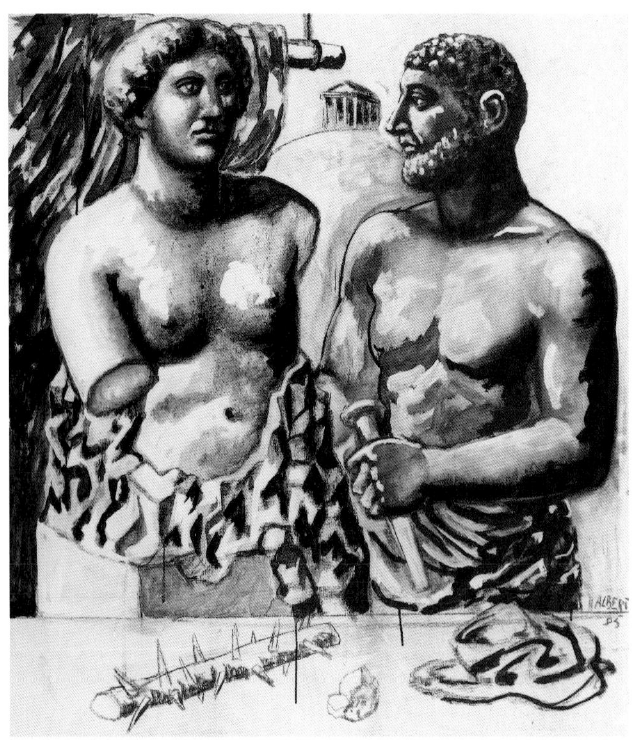

2. *The Sculptor*, 1985

Although it's true that I'm an expert, I don't really know what "painting" is. I use my own painting exclusively as a means of clarifying something . . . to myself, too. What's more, I'm not at all interested in the question of which style is dominant at the moment. My physical work is a means of transporation—the painting is something I have to develop myself. I refuse to be dictated to. People used to demand beauty, grandeur, and suchlike from works of art; later they wanted the opposite, and that's a form of dictatorship, too. There are a great many artists who maintain that there are some things "you just can't do anymore these days." I can tell you a personal story about that. In the summer of 1972 I was in Florence for awhile, and one weekend I went on a trip to the mountains with some colleagues. We got out of the car and there we were standing in the Tuscan countryside, with the cypress trees, the olive groves, and the old houses—it was all harmony for us. The sun was setting and soon it was out of sight, but the rays of sunlight were still illuminating the countryside obliquely, the shadows were getting longer and longer, and you could sense the approach of nightfall although it was really still daytime. We stood there, with our own consciousness, looking at this dramatic spectacle, and suddenly one of us said, "It's a pity you can't paint that anymore these days." That had been the key word I'd heard since I started trying to be a painter. And I said to him, out of pure impudence, "Why can't you? You can do everything." It was only after I'd said it that I realized that what had initially just been a piece of provocation was really true. Why should anyone tell me I can't paint a sunset? I saw how reduced we had already become in our perceptions: we couldn't look at a sunset impartially because it might expose us to the danger of possibly painting it one day—and that's forbidden. It was probably at that period that I withdrew from the common experience of feelings. When I replied to my colleague out of a desire to oppose him, actually I was replying to myself.

Excerpt from "Conversation between the Painter Hermann Albert and the Author Klaus Thiele-Dorhmann." Reprinted from Raab Galerie, Berlin, and Sander Gallery, New York, *Hermann Albert: Paintings 1983-84*, (1984). Used by permission.

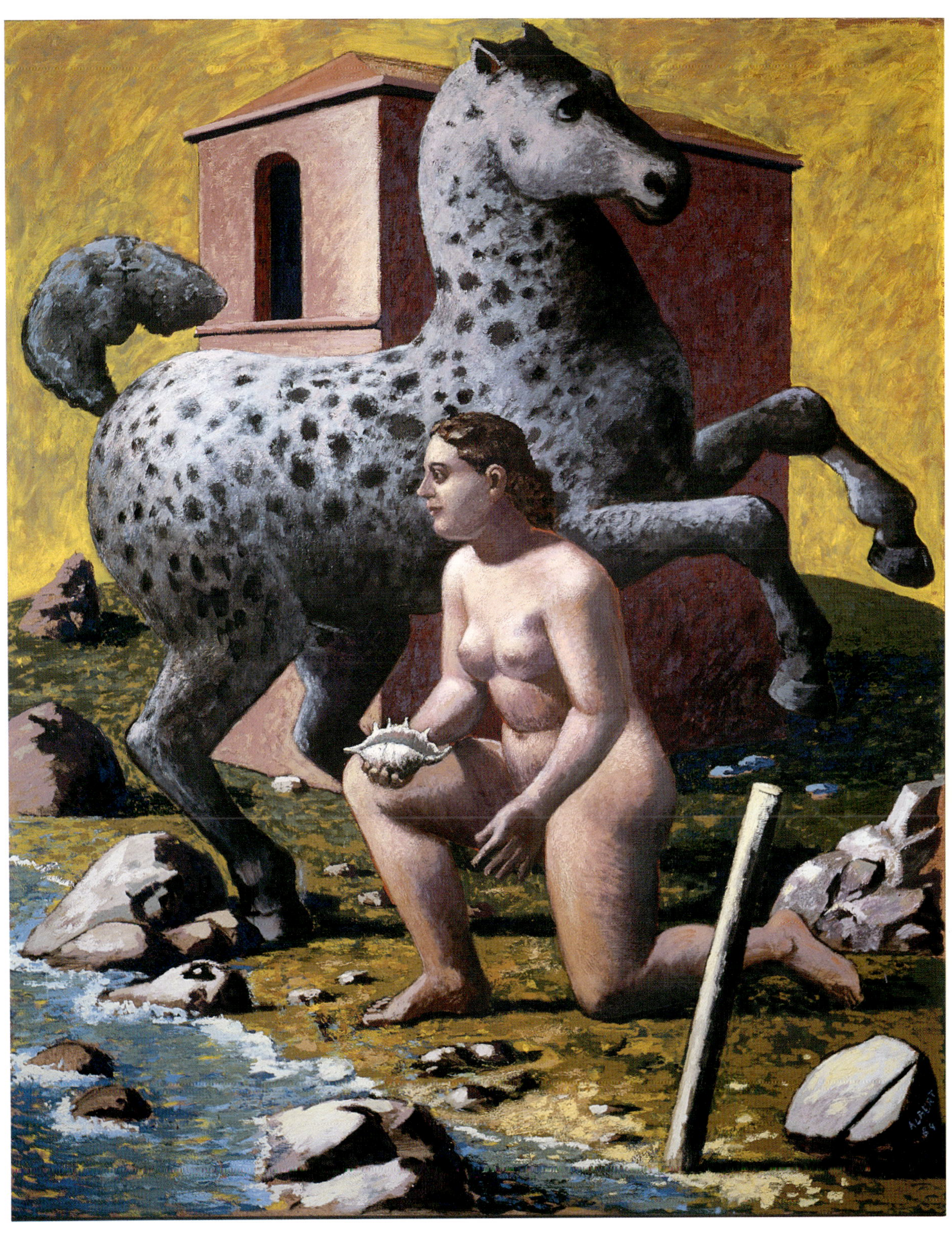

1. *Pferd und Akt am Meer (Der Abend)*, 1984

Edward Allington

In 1816 Lord Elgin, that most admirable thief, gave his collection of sculpture to the British nation, which received them with characteristic meanness and disinterest. As was customary at the time (it being considered that neither expert nor public would appreciate the sight of headless, armless, and otherwise mutilated statues), Lord Elgin approached Antonio Canova to undertake the required restoration. Canova refused, saying, we are told, that although it was to be lamented that these statues should have suffered so much due to the process of time and barbarism, it was undeniable that they were the untouched works of the ablest artists the world had ever seen, and that it would be sacrilege for him or any other sculptor to touch them with a chisel.

Sisyphus, who Homer informs us was the wisest and most prudent of mortals, was nonetheless condemned by the gods for having practiced a certain levity towards them, stealing their secrets, and for having put death in chains. For these crimes they sentenced him to the most dreadful of punishments—to ceaselessly push a rock up a mountain only to have it roll down again of its own weight—and condemned him to an eternity of futile and hopeless labor.

As Albert Camus states, Sisyphus is the absurd hero, and due to this very absurdity, the myth is also a figure for the state of art today. I am by nature a classicist, someone whose first remembered story is Homer's *Iliad,* whose first youthful notion of beauty was formed by Greek art, and whose early inquiry, what is the good?, was met in Greek philosophy. I tend to see things primarily in relation to what I know of the classics; itself a seemingly absurd position. I do not talk of that most tragic of conditions, neoclassicism, which is merely advanced nostalgia, usually grossly misinformed. Ancient Greece was not a Golden Age. For me with classical reference there is no nostalgia; it is more than a mode, a basis for thinking, a starting point.

The real issue is ethical, relating to how one chooses to conduct one's life as an artist. Today every artist has the liberty (an extreme limitation as it's easier to break rules than to make them) to reassemble the language of art afresh, since without any rigid criteria there can be no

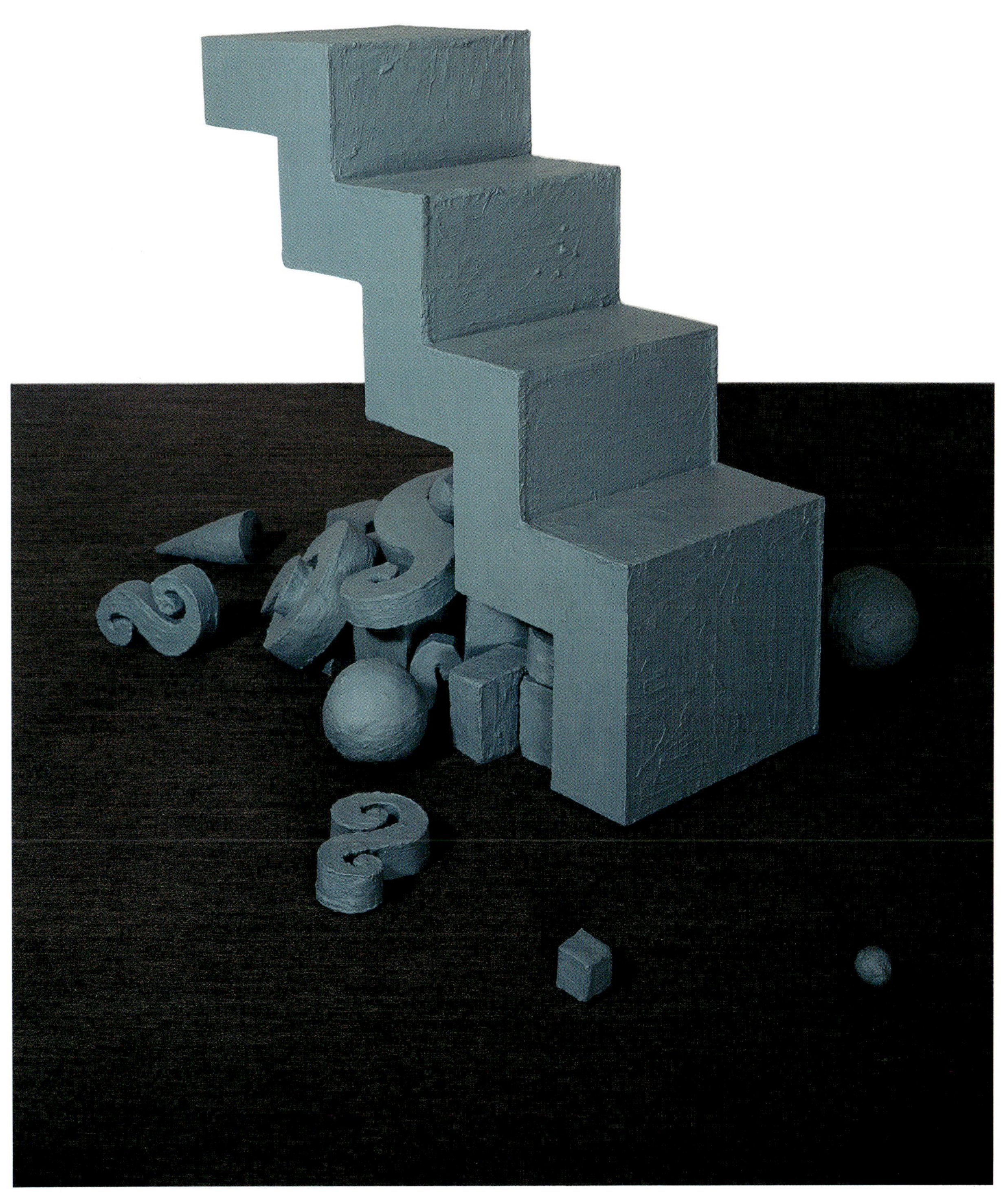

5.   *Three and Four Steps*, 1986

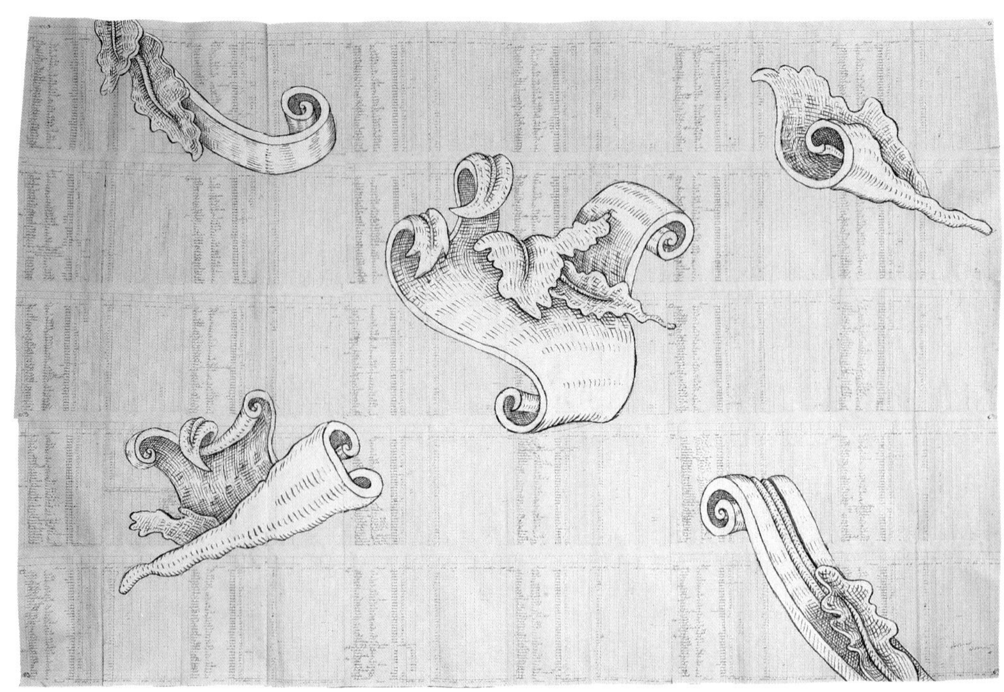

3. *Decorative Fragments*, 1986

a priori criteria (taste is not an a priori crite-rion). So that which artists gain in self-expression, they lose in terms of order. Which is why I find it instructive to look to the Greeks, or even the Egyptians, for they had a canon of beauty so-called that was by definition con-tained within the rules of their tradition; a tra-dition that was developed so that it eventually caused artists of the Renaissance to claim title to a status higher than artisanship, to break with the guilds. This independence was based on the virtue of them having to be conversant with logic, poetry, and reason to articulate rules of perspective and manipulate the levels of reference within the work. This century saw the breaking of such long-standing standards.

It is no coincidence that when the post-impressionists decided that art was the realm of sensation and emotion rather than reason that art lost its role to other media. (I do not denigrate them by saying this. They liberated art from decaying order, yet inadvertently con-demned it to wild beauty of chaos.) Sculpture died the same death; Rodin is the tragic and pathetic last breath from the already-mortified corpse.

Edward Allington, 1986

18

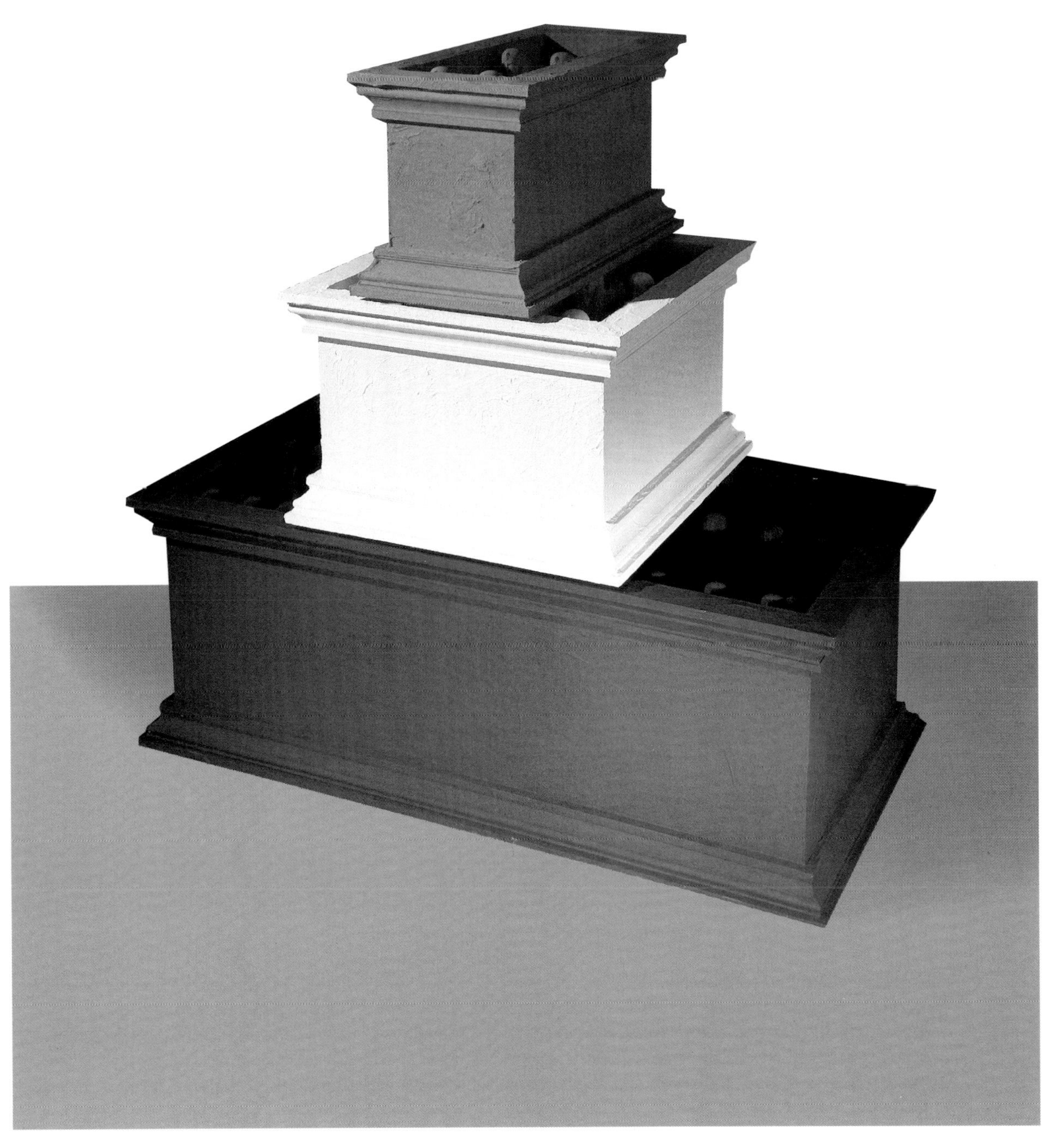

4.   *The Past Recycled: Metropolitan Egypt*, 1986

Siah Armajani

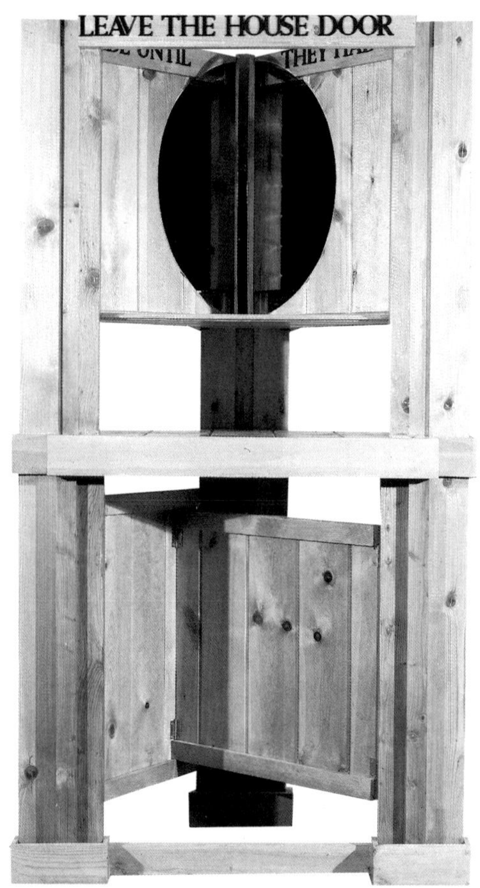

7. *Dictionary for Building: Fireplace Mantle with Windows*, 1982–83

It is the room that allows the chair to be, and being at hand manifests understanding of the room in relationship to the chair. The room is not the sum of the things which built it into a room. It is conditioned by every object in it. But if it were not for the room the objects would not be there. The totality of instruments becomes the only possiblity for existence of an instrument. The room lets the chair "be" by bringing it into instrumental totality, by centering it around some zero point. Letting it "be" is discovered by being at hand and through encounters. Architecture/sculpture is the means for humans to measure distances between things, to reach objects and to encounter them. One does not encounter things only theoretically but through activity, investigation, and management prior to one's knowledge of things. "Practical activity has its own sort of vision." (Heidegger) The relationship between the front and back door of a house is within our activity. It is our activity that embraces these two distant and separate entities. Practical activity is not "atheoretical."

Excerpt from "Notes 1973-1977" by Siah Armajani. Reprinted from Philadelphia College of Art, *Siah Armajani: Red School House for Thomas Paine* (1978), by Janet Kardon, pp. 12-13. Used by permission.

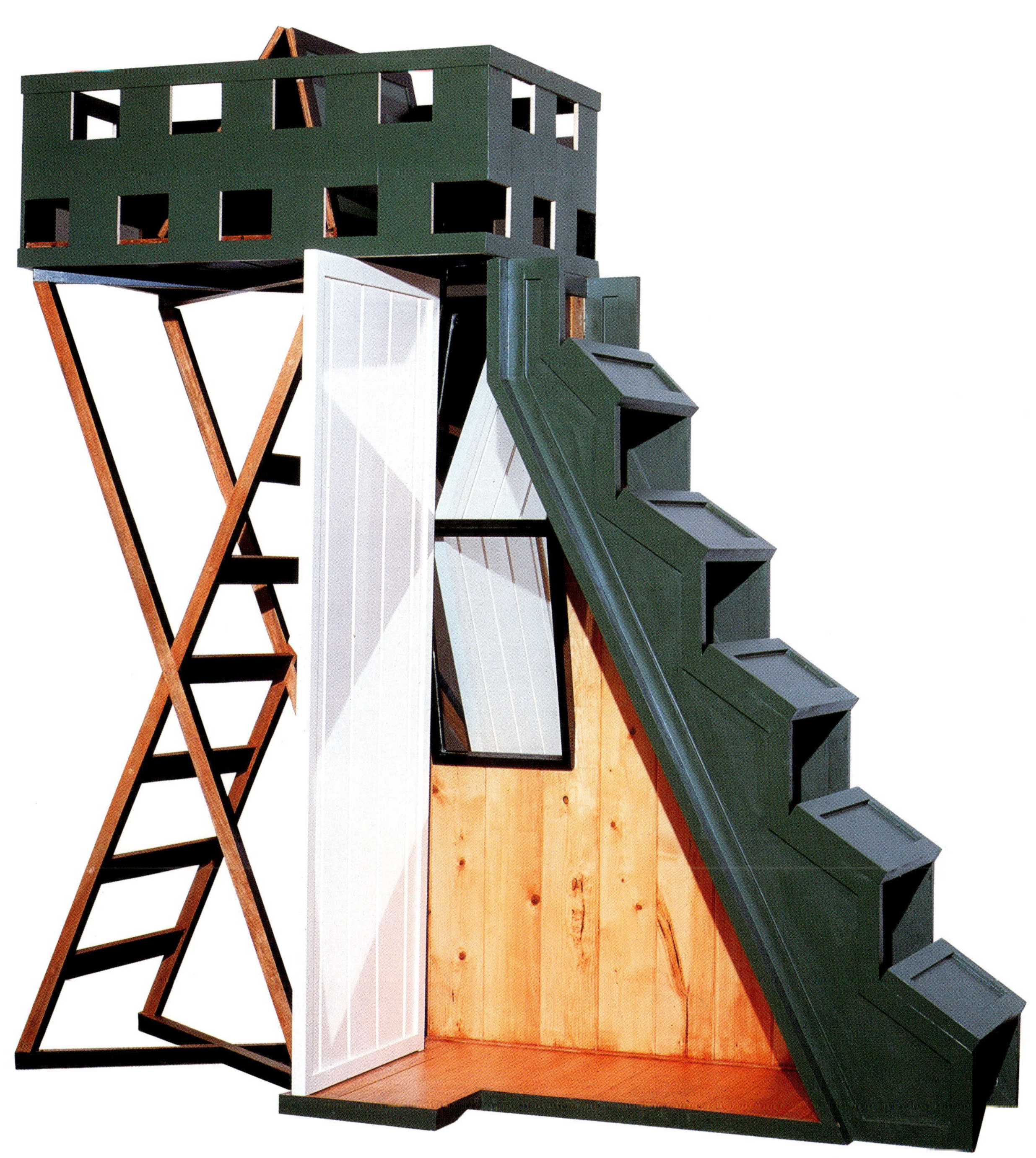

8.   *Dictionary for Building: Closet Under Landing*, 1985

Roger Brown

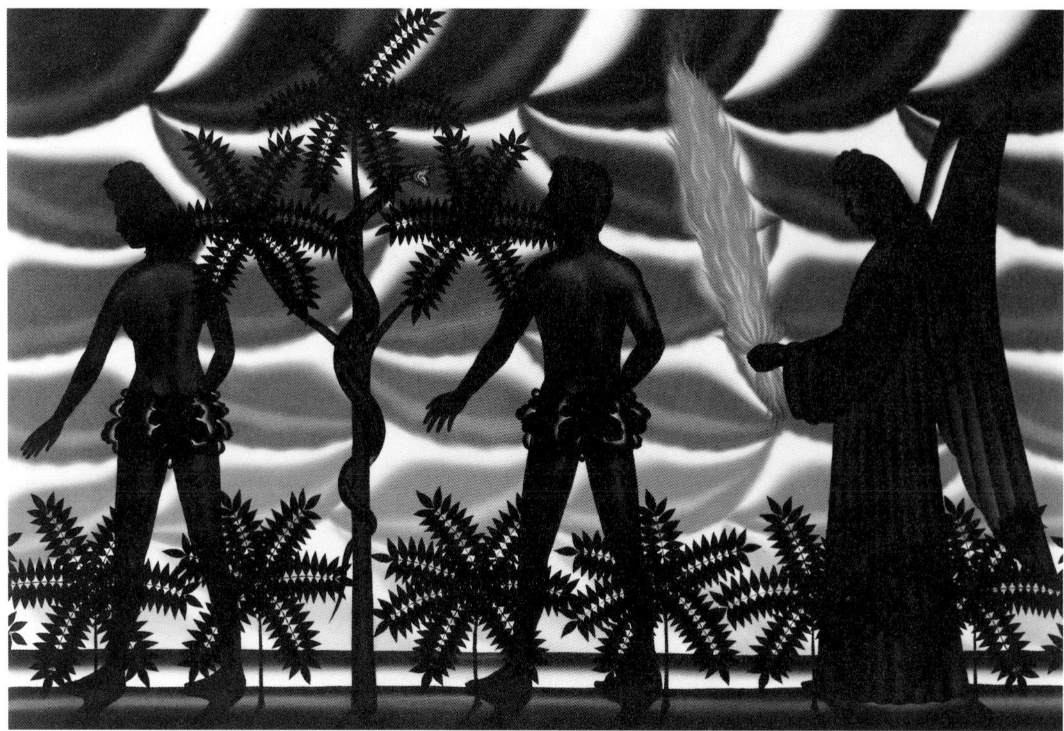

9.   *Adam and Eve (Expulsion from the Garden)*, 1982

The Biblical stories, like the Greek myths, are a part of our own culture. No matter which Protestant, Catholic, or Jewish religion one was taught, those stories became a part of what formed most of us from children into adults. This is even more true with the Biblical stories than with the Greek myths. However, in this age it is more popular for artists to refer to the Greek classics than to the Bible. I am interested in the Biblical stories as the myths of our own culture; therefore, as subjects for paintings.

I am not only interested in Biblical stories as subjects for paintings. In fact, only six or eight paintings out of the four hundred or so I have completed in the last eighteen years have had Biblical subjects. I am also interested in popular culture and the vernacular—whether it be architecture, artifacts, comic books, or utilitarian objects. The galvanized garbage can with its fluted, tapered sides has struck me for a long time as a parody of an upside-down Doric column. The idea was dormant for a number of years, when finally I decided to merge the garbage can and galvanized gutter with corrugated sheet metal into a garbage-can Parthenon or "Galvanized Temple." Otherwise, the part art history has played in my own work has been one of showing me how to present any number of visual representations. The content or subject of my work has always come from the present or from my own experience. I learned from the early Renaissance and Oriental artists how to structure space on a flat surface. I learned from African and Oceanic art how to use pattern and stylization to create my own effects. I learned from naive and folk artists to deal with my own world and to offer my own limitations as myself.

Roger Brown, 1986

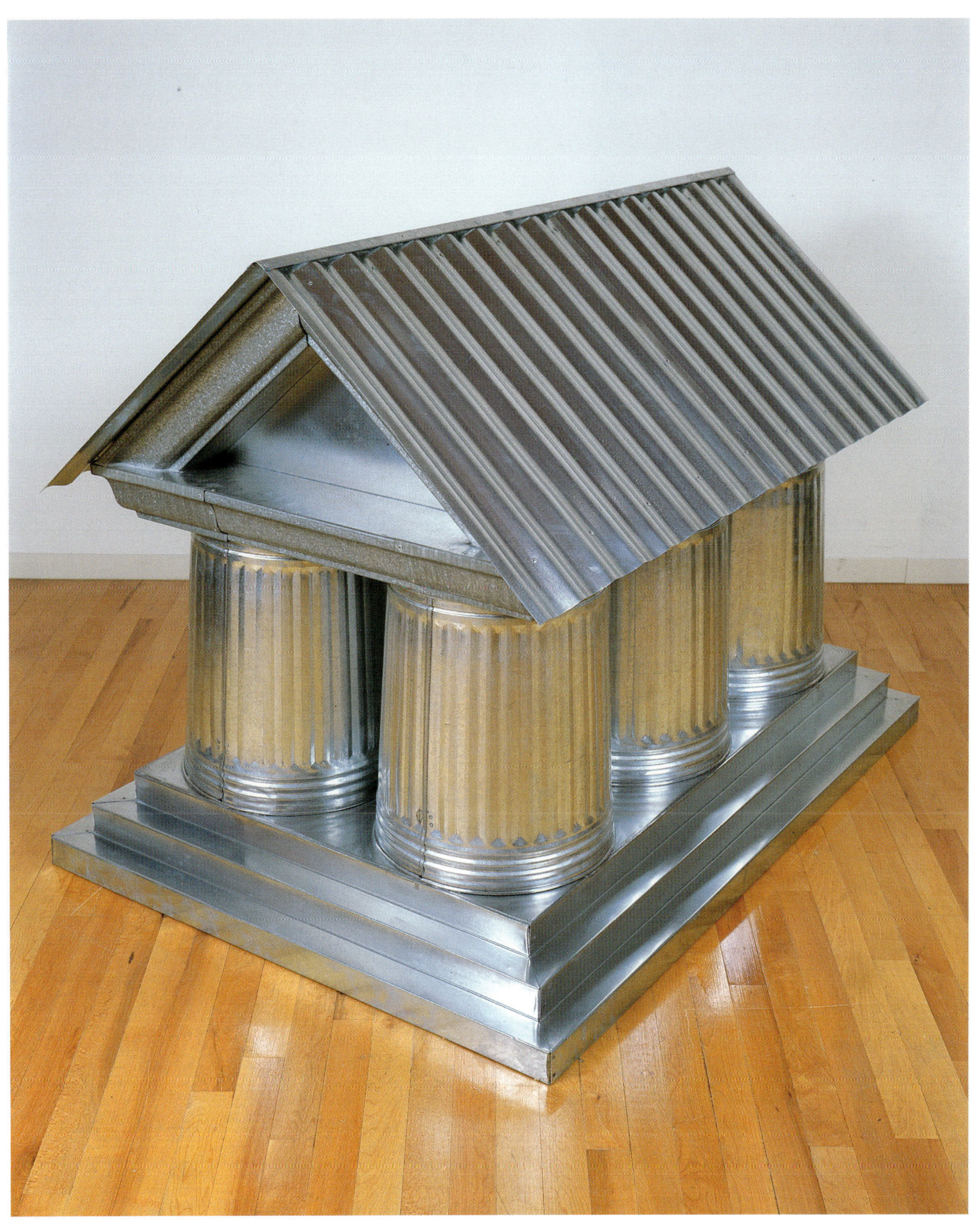

10. *Galvanized Temple*, 1985

Harry Fritzius

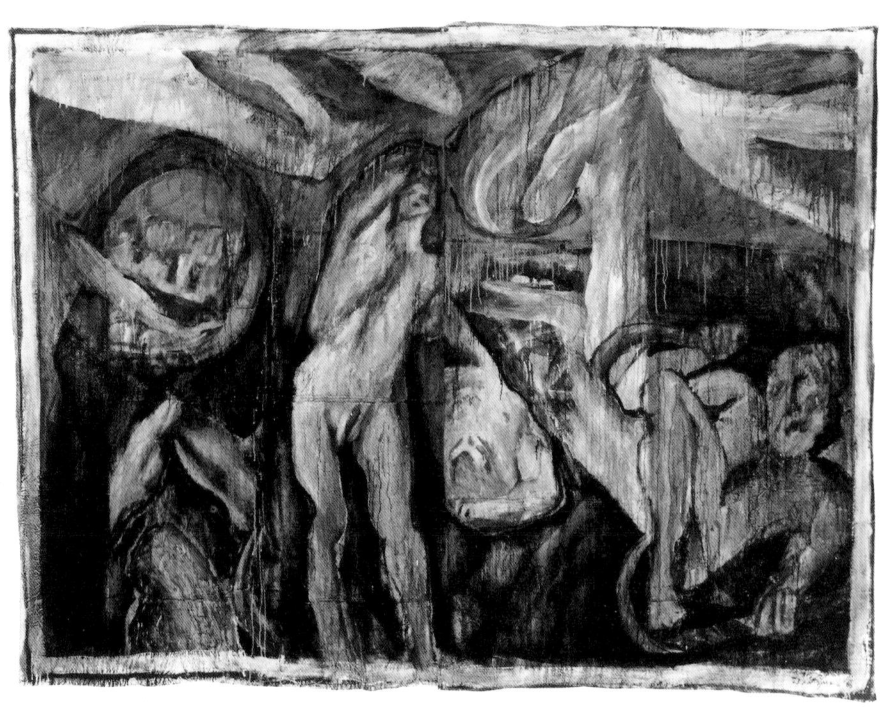

13.   *Laocoön after El Greco*, 1986

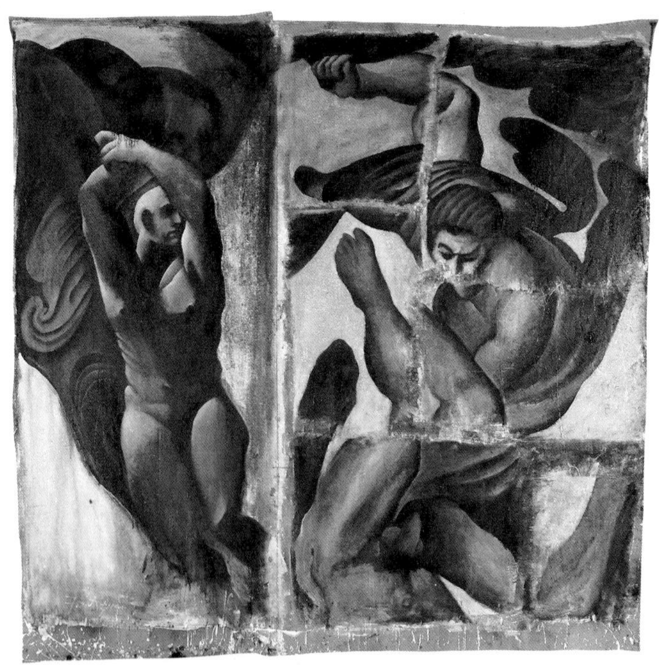

11.   *Michelangelo after the Sistine Chapel No. 1*, 1985

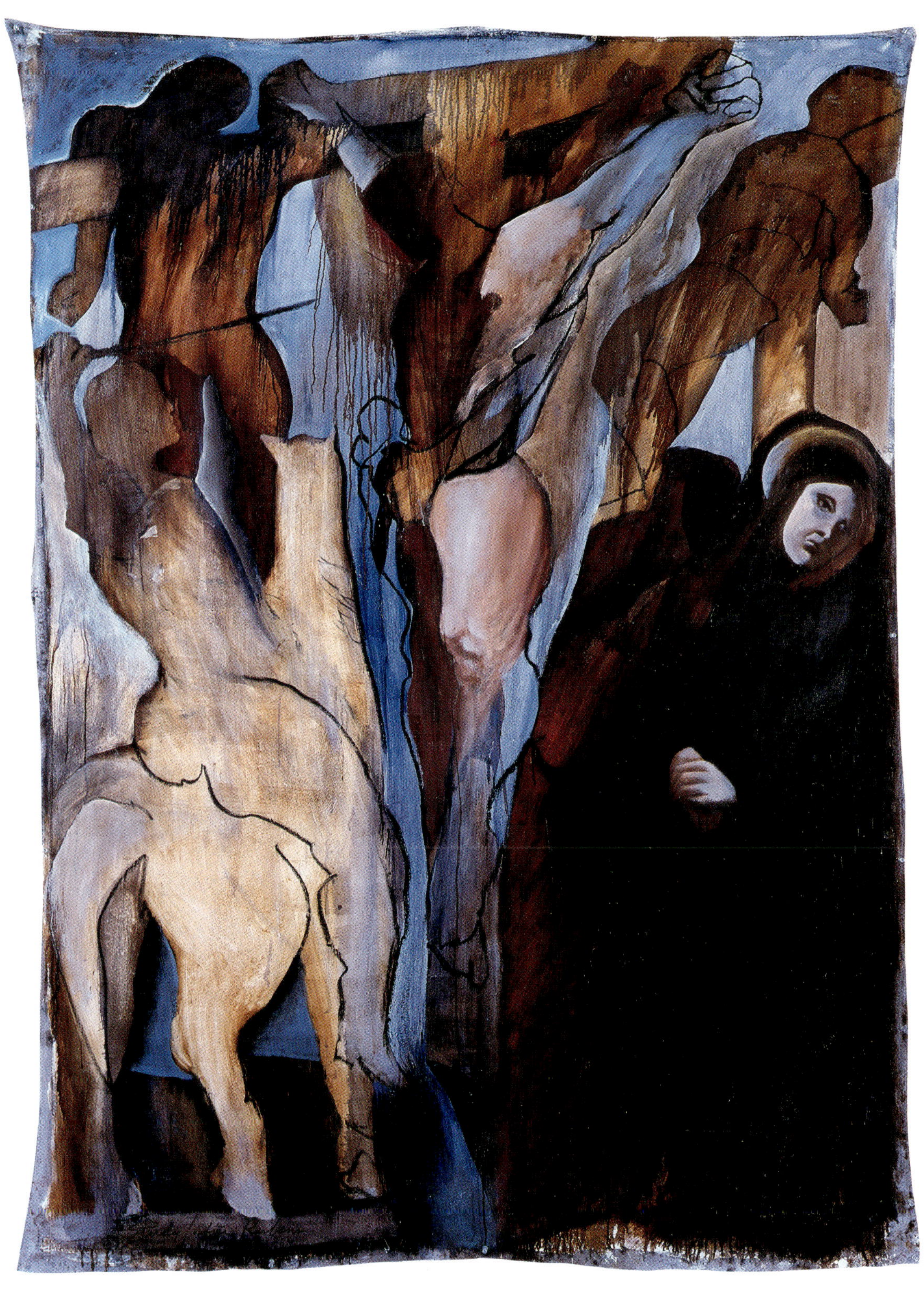

12.   *Study after Rubens*, 1985

Douglas Higgins

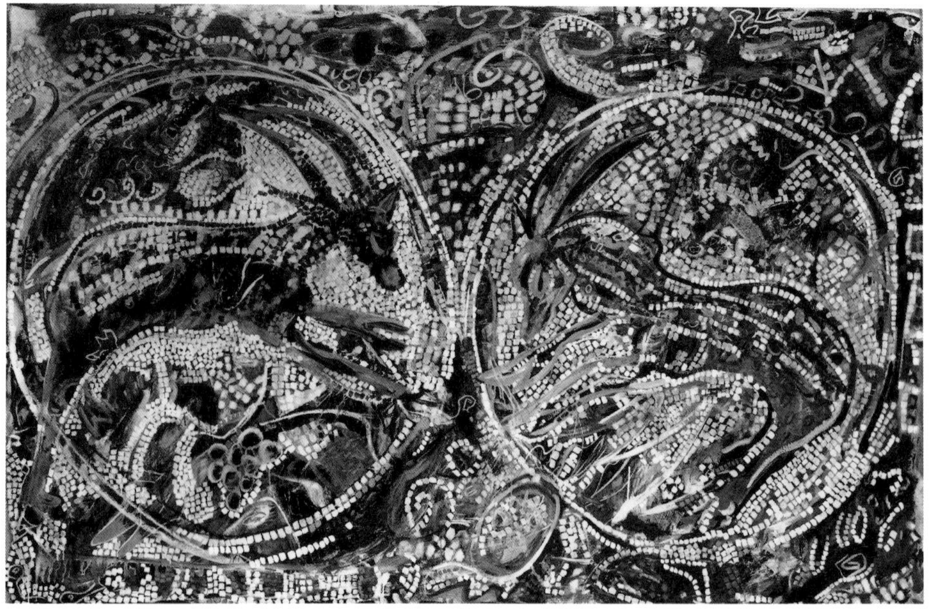

15.   *Rams of Asarkaya*, 1985

Central to my work since 1978 has been an involvement with the ability of graphic images, icons, and symbols (whether significant and universal or peculiar and cryptic) to portray culture as a continuity where past and present are overlapping, fused, and simultaneous. Much like culture, my images are built one layer upon another, one inspired by, one indebted to the other.

In the studio my affinity with this phenomenon (now deeply imbedded) energizes the activity in a curious way, as if some genetic memory has been engaged. Portraying this continuity as sometimes eloquent, sometimes awkward, and rarely predictable requires an exhausting amount of acceptance of self-trust. At times failure seems assured, as images wrestle and strain for identities, their placement never arbitrary but rather inevitable, irreversible. I don't consciously make a decision between using what has been or what is "of the moment," only a distinction between what seems continuous and what does not.

My paintings are what you might call an entropic cascade where all gathers—past, present, and future. It's what T. S. Eliot calls "the still point of the turning world," or for Philip Guston, the "condition of continuity" for the "subversion of an intolerable finality."

Douglas Higgins, 1986

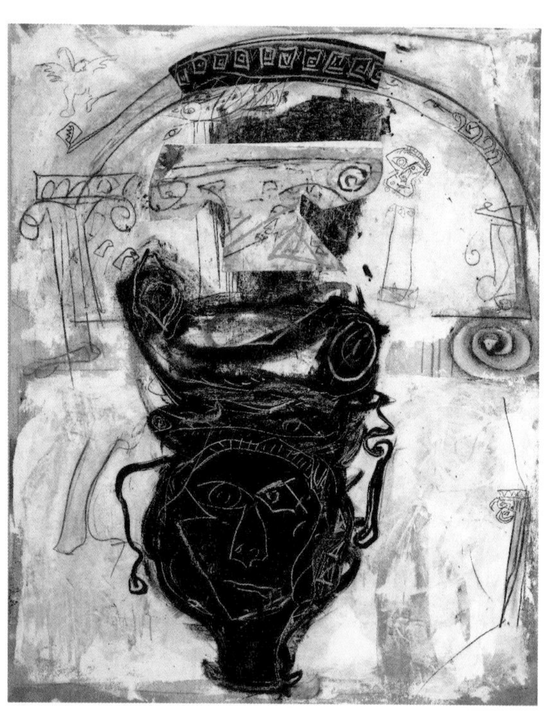

14.   *Prometheus*, 1984

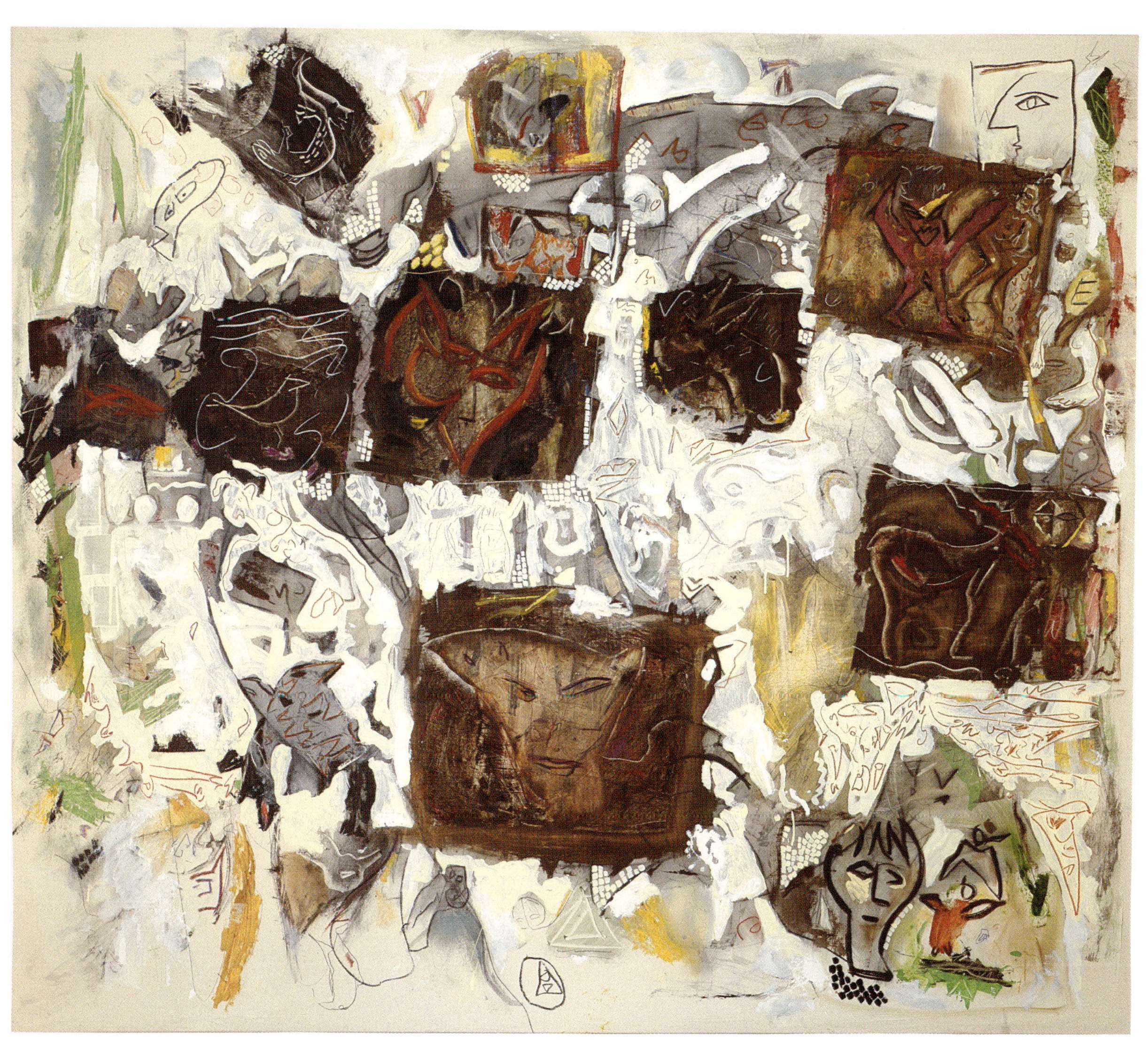

16.   *Melancholia (after Dürer)*, 1986

David Hollowell

The most obvious reason the paintings of Piero della Francesca and Andrea del Sarto appear in my painting *La Galleria* is to pay homage to their greatness. The reason I selected the four particular images to appear on the walls in *La Galleria* is difficult to explain, primarily because what I had hoped to achieve by incorporating these images with a more traditional form (women in leotards) came from an instinctual sense, a felt experience, not one that was rational and/or premeditated.

Actually, the painting probably would never have come about if I had not had the opportunity to witness the small chapel in the building located in Florence on Cavour Street, number 69. The chapel has its entire interior frescoed with images painted by Andrea del Sarto of John the Baptist's life. This interior undoubtedly was the inspiration for *La Galleria*. This space has a smell to it, a persistent silence, and an incredibly soft light. I wanted my painting to capture the essence of this experience.

David Hollowell, 1986

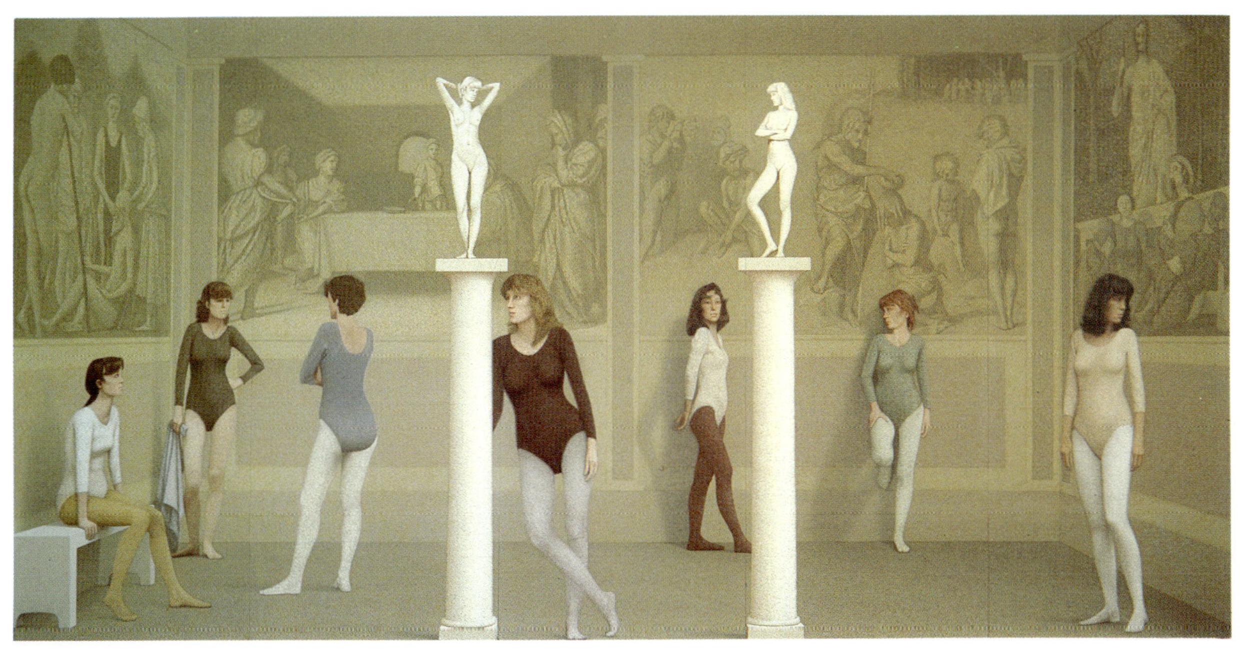

17.   *La Galleria*, 1985

Komar and Melamid

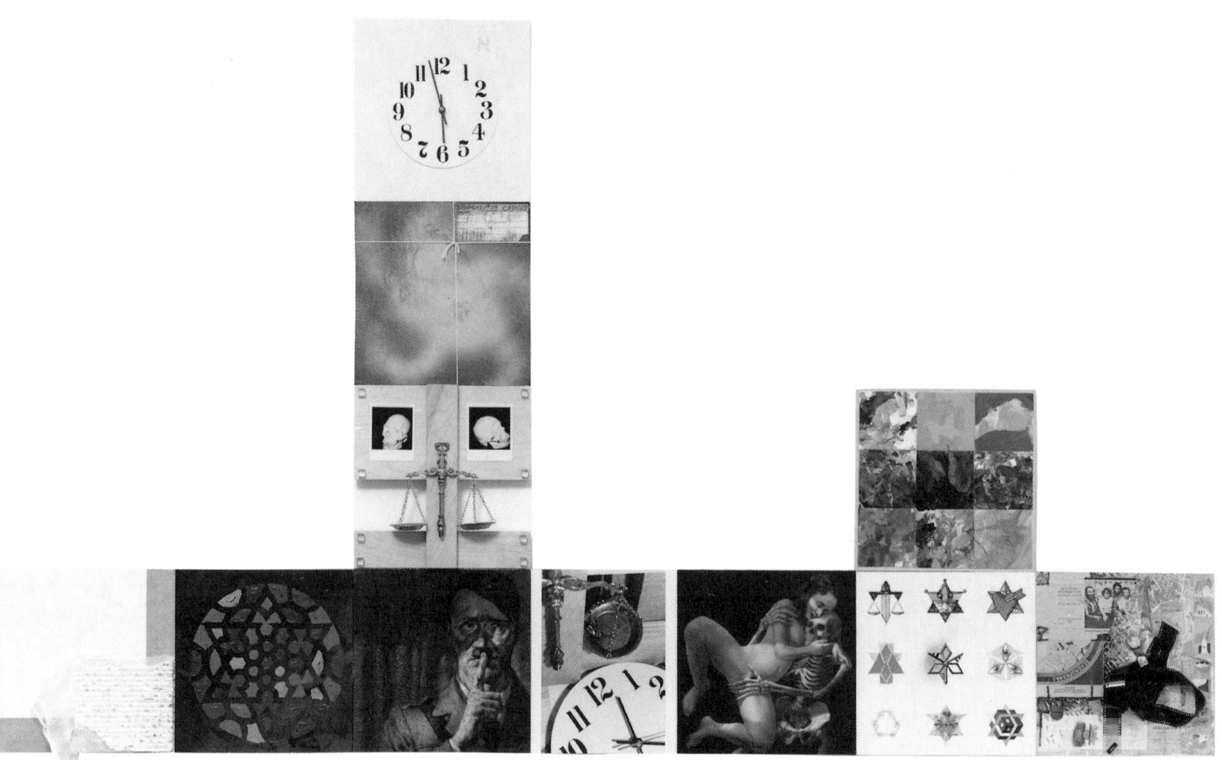

20.   *When I Was a Child Matzoh Reminded Me of a Braille Book*, 1984–85

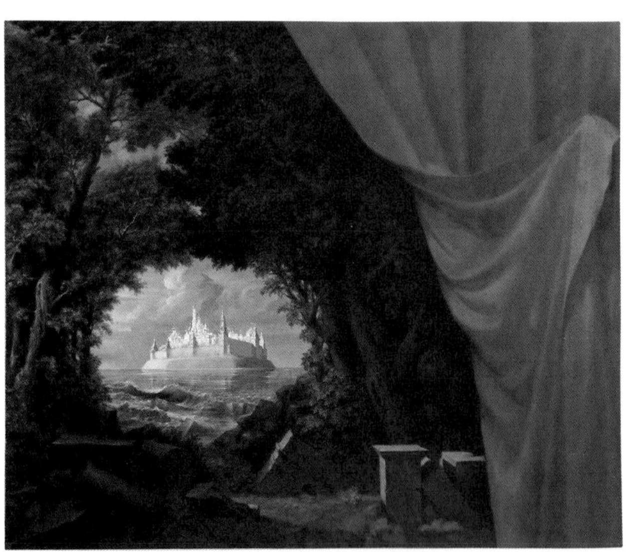

18.   *Nostalgic View of the Kremlin from Manhattan*, 1981–82

Usually artists arrive at a trademark and then they're stuck with it. I think we found a new possibility. I don't know what the result will be, but...how to call it, "style," or manner, how to call when you change...now I think you can speak of intonation instead. Because we can say the same thing, but with a different intonation. We can use the same work, but change intonation. Style sometimes is simply intonation. You can work in Cezanne's style, Rembrandt's...because formal searches, it's like a book: children use a book with many letters, and the whole alphabet is there. But in the twentieth century, with formal searches, people found the whole book. Impressionist, Expressionist, Cubist, Surrealist—a lot of formal possiblities, but it's empty now, because it's possible to use all of them. A line you can make like this, or a stroke like that...now all these books are empty. Nobody can find a new letter for this alphabet. If you find one, that's okay.

Excerpt from "Komar & Melamid: An interview with Gary Indiana," by Gary Indiana. Reprinted from *El Passeante* (Spain) (Winter 1986). Used by permission.

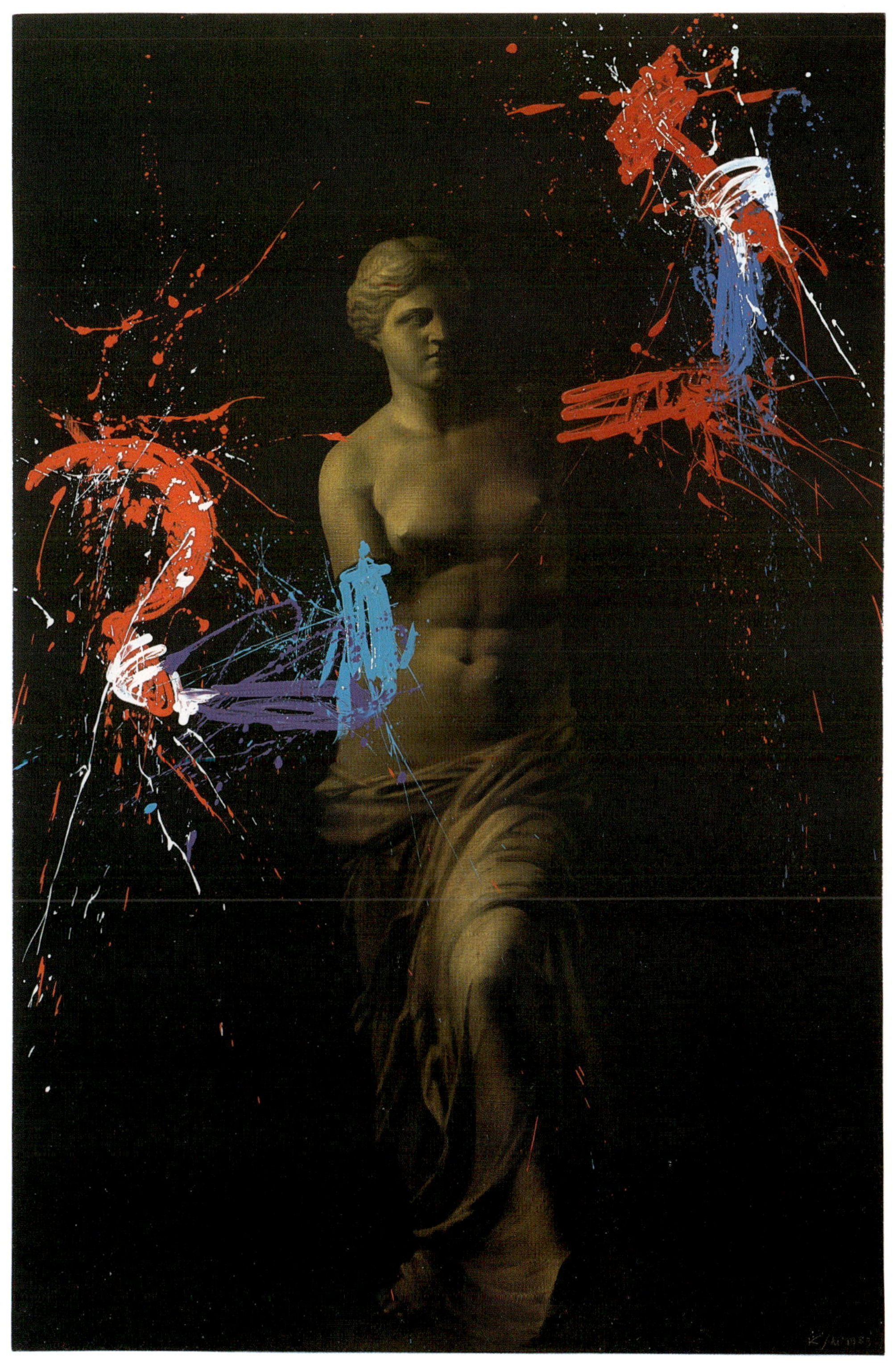

19.   *Venus of Milo,* 1983

Christopher Le Brun

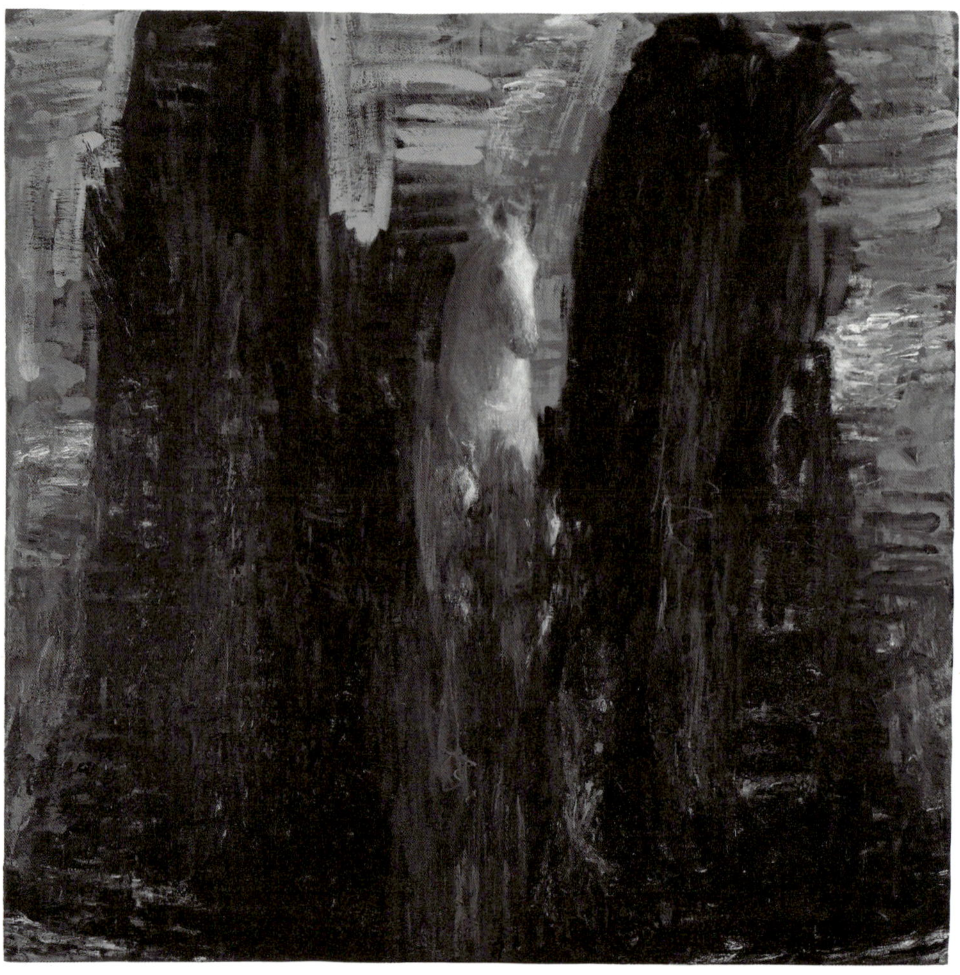

21. *Prow*, 1983

Le Brun's paintings are full of echoes. The early abstract works became Neoclassical and Symbolist landscapes, borrowed from Claude and Böcklin. The horses in the recent works, themselves laden with associations, trot, plunge, or fly through landscapes which are forested with symbols—often the cypresses, towers, and rocks derived from Böcklin. There are hints of battles, storms and fire, Turneresque passages, and streaming banners reminiscent of Delacroix. Nature is seen through art. Le Brun's imagination is fed by the visions of others. In this he is of the moment. His horse image in the landscape, which draws on Neoclassicism, Symbolism, Romanticism, and Abstract Expressionism, among other sources, is a potent image for the struggle between the abstract and the figurative which he sees as the "almost pathological post-modernist condition." His Romanticism might fit with Baudelaire's definition: a "mode of feeling" which touches on the "epic side of modern life." Le Brun's 1982 exhibition, with its themes of heroism and battle, was showing during the Falkland's crisis and at the time much was made of this coincidence. The true struggle is in the attempt to make continuity out of dislocation.

Excerpt from "White Horses…Christopher Le Brun," by Caroline Collier. Reprinted from *Studio International*, vol. 198, no. 1010 (1985), pp. 14-17. Used by permission.

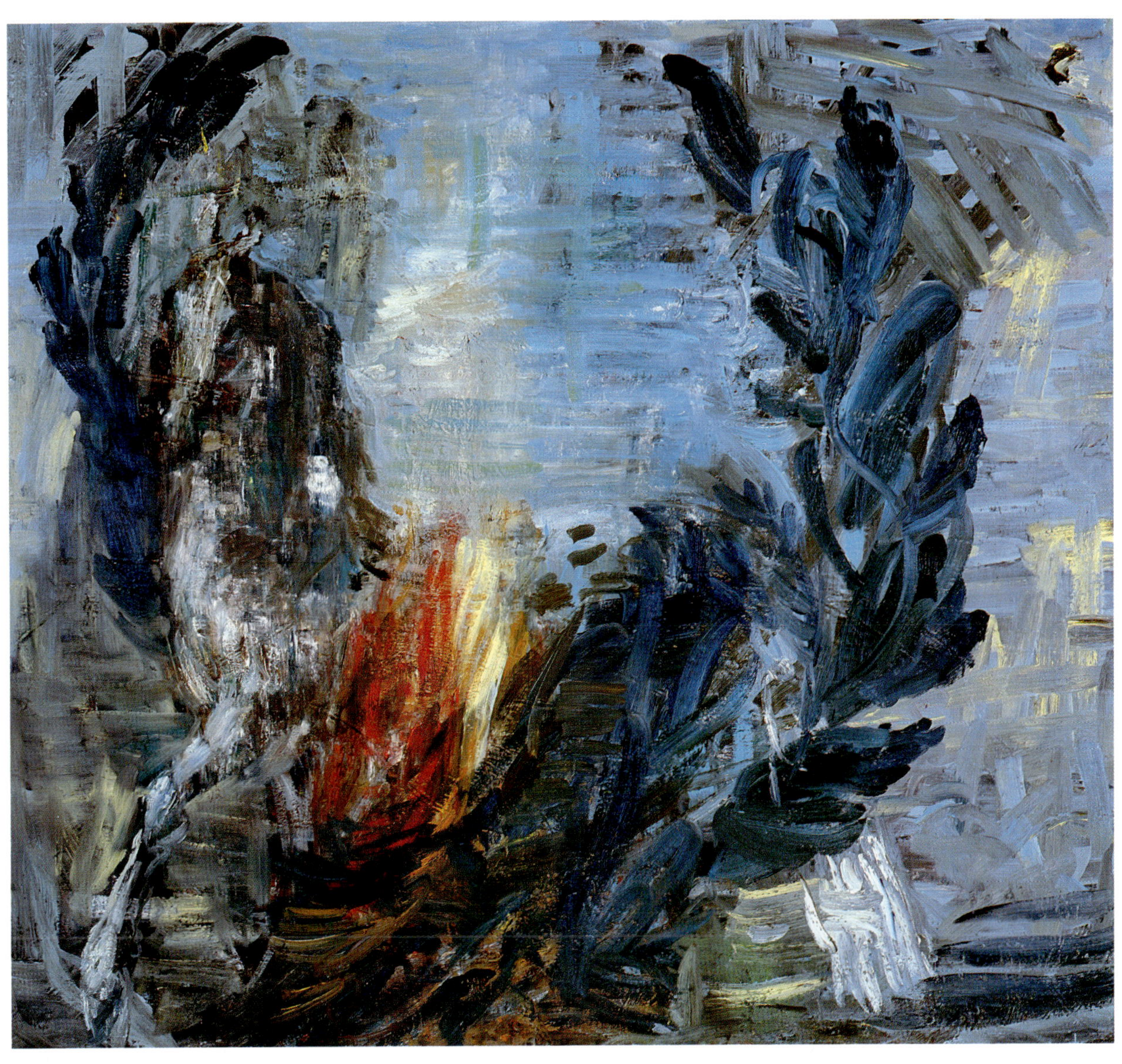

22.   *Wreath*, 1983

Carlo Maria Mariani

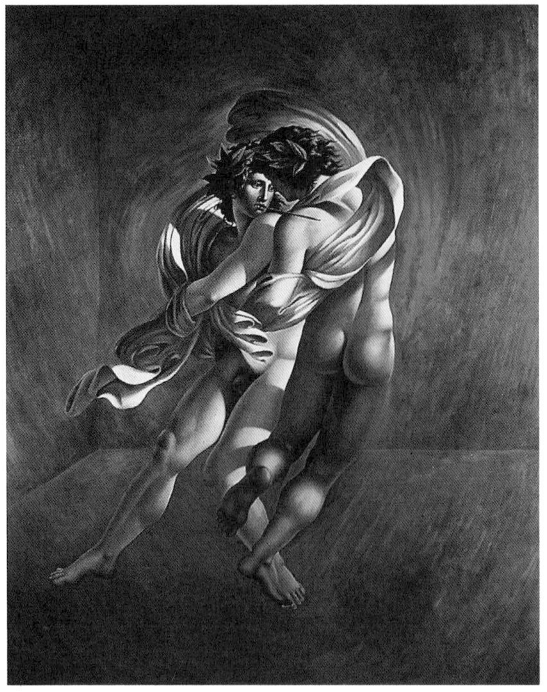

25. *Guardarsi in uno specchio celeste
(Looking into a Celestial Mirror)*, 1984

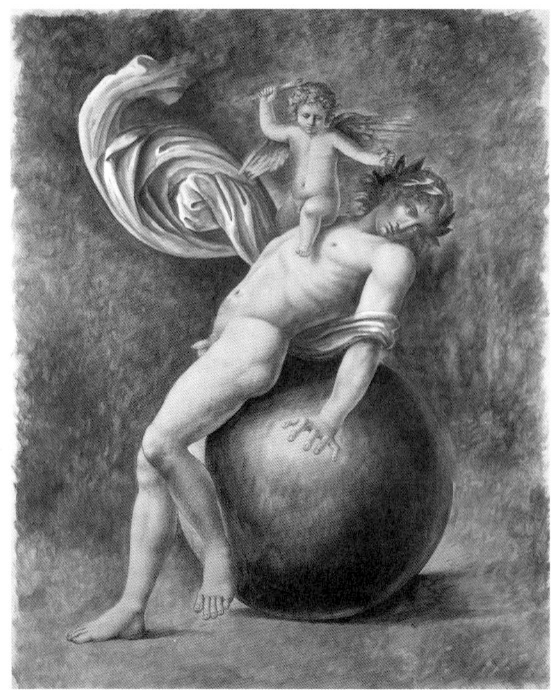

24. *Ecco sei tu, Eletto*, 1983

CMM: I was fascinated by the artists of the cin-
quecento—Tintoretto, the Venitians in general. Later on by Caravaggio.

DB: Everybody loves Caravaggio. There are
four or five works within three blocks of
your studio.

CMM: Then I lived in another part of Rome. I
would say that my Neoclassic style began
around ten years ago.

DB: Influenced by an event or circumstance?

CMM: No, I came to this period after years of
research in libraries. I read much literature of
the period, especially Winckelmann. I got
some ideas to do some research myself.

DB: Imaginary archaeology?

CMM: Yes.

DB: I see these cold masks and sculpturelike
figures in your work. Do they hide some mes-
sage or sentiment? Or are they just forms and
subjects?

CMM: They are, but more than forms and subjects they are an attempt at the aesthetics of
beauty. That attracts me very much.

DB: Are they usually imaginary figures or are
they drawn from life?

CMM: No, no, the real does not interest me.
They are suggested to me by fantasy or by certain Classical iconography, especially Greek
statuary. That is my source.

Excerpt from "Carlo Maria Mariani in his Studio in
Rome: An Interview," by Danny Berger. Reprinted from
Print Collector's Newsletter (July-August 1984), pp. 84-87.
Used by permission.

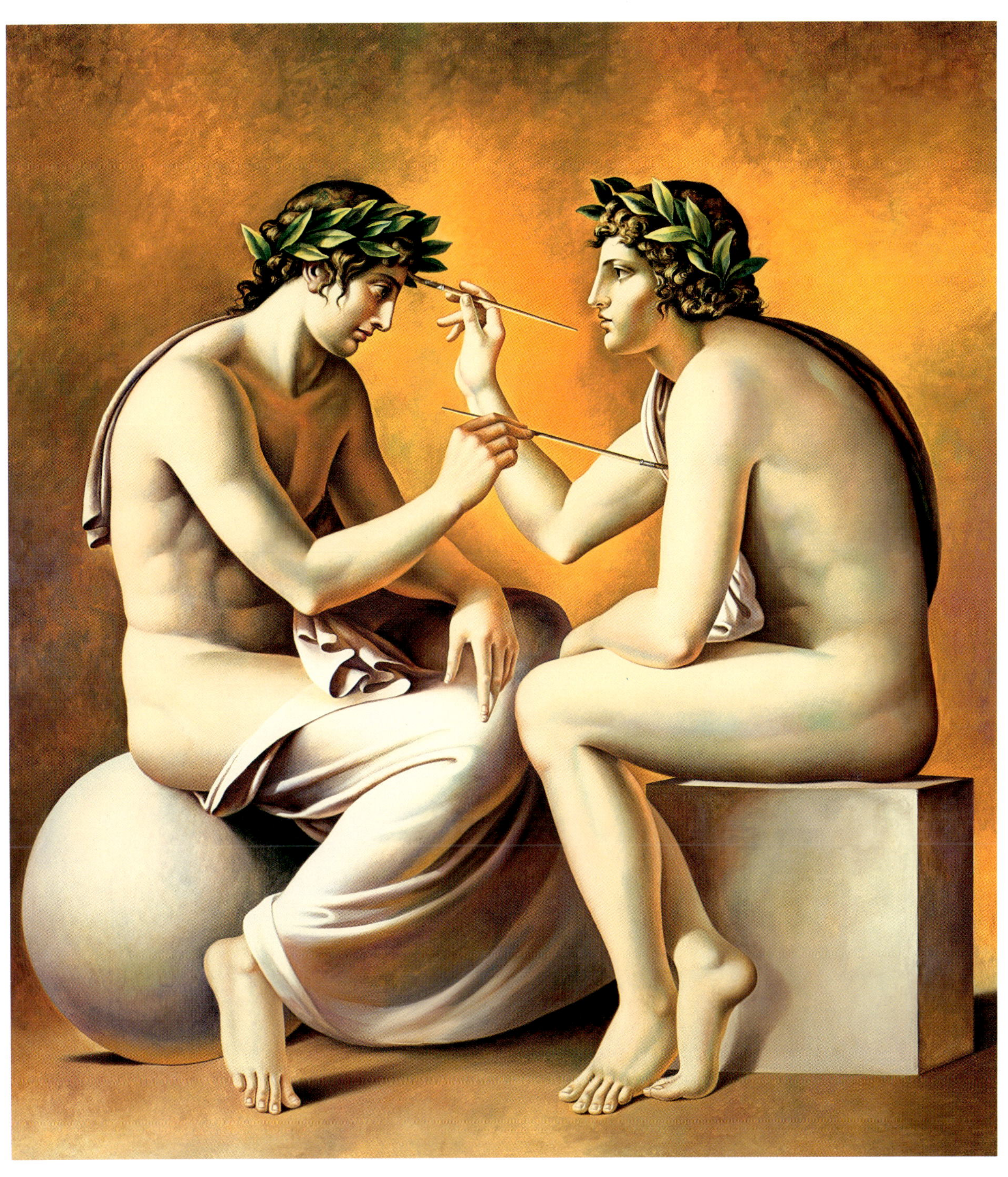

23.   *La Mano Ubbidisce all'Intelletto (The Hand Submits to the Intellect)*, 1983

Ann McCoy

The images presented in the works have their origins in dreams, in the collective unconscious. They are obtained through an ancient process called "incubation," a "sleeping in." In the classical world, incubation was practiced at 412 sanctuaries, the most famous being Epidaurus and Kos. Dreams were known to be therapeutic in nature, to bring about healings of spiritual, psychological, and physical ills.

In the modern world, with its emphasis on materialism and extroversion, the self-healing process connected with dream symbolism is overlooked by many and has been relegated to psychoanalysis. The chief practitioner of the process of relating dream symbolism to religion and healing was C. G. Jung. The American Indian is one of the few races that has not lost track of this natural process. The Chippewa feel that the dream is still the most important source of information and knowledge. Dreams are still acknowledged to be the realm of revelation and transformation. The dream world, the collective unconscious, is an autonomous complex that joins the individual to the psychic reservoir of human history and experience. It is inherent in our genetic structure and possesses an intelligence of its own.

The images in the works first appeared in a series of dreams. They are not appropriated in the usual postmodernist sense. After I catalogue the dreams, they are researched and traced through the world's literature. As series that I feel have personal or philosophical importance emerge, they are grouped in the drawings. The actual making of the artworks is the end product of the process.

The work entitled *Pyramid for Martin Hurson* shows the inner chamber of the pyramid of Unas at Saqqara. The grave, which has appeared often in my dreams, is a symbol of Putrefactio, the rotting of organic bodies. The Putrefactio is the first stage of the alchemical Great Work. Much of the alchemical Great Work has its roots in the prototype of Osiris. The old man (king) is dismembered, decomposes, and is reconstituted as the spiritual man, who is incorruptible and eternal. The myth has its parallel in a process that occurs in the depths of the psyche. Since much of alchemical literature relates to Egyptian funerary practices, the pyramid interior became a

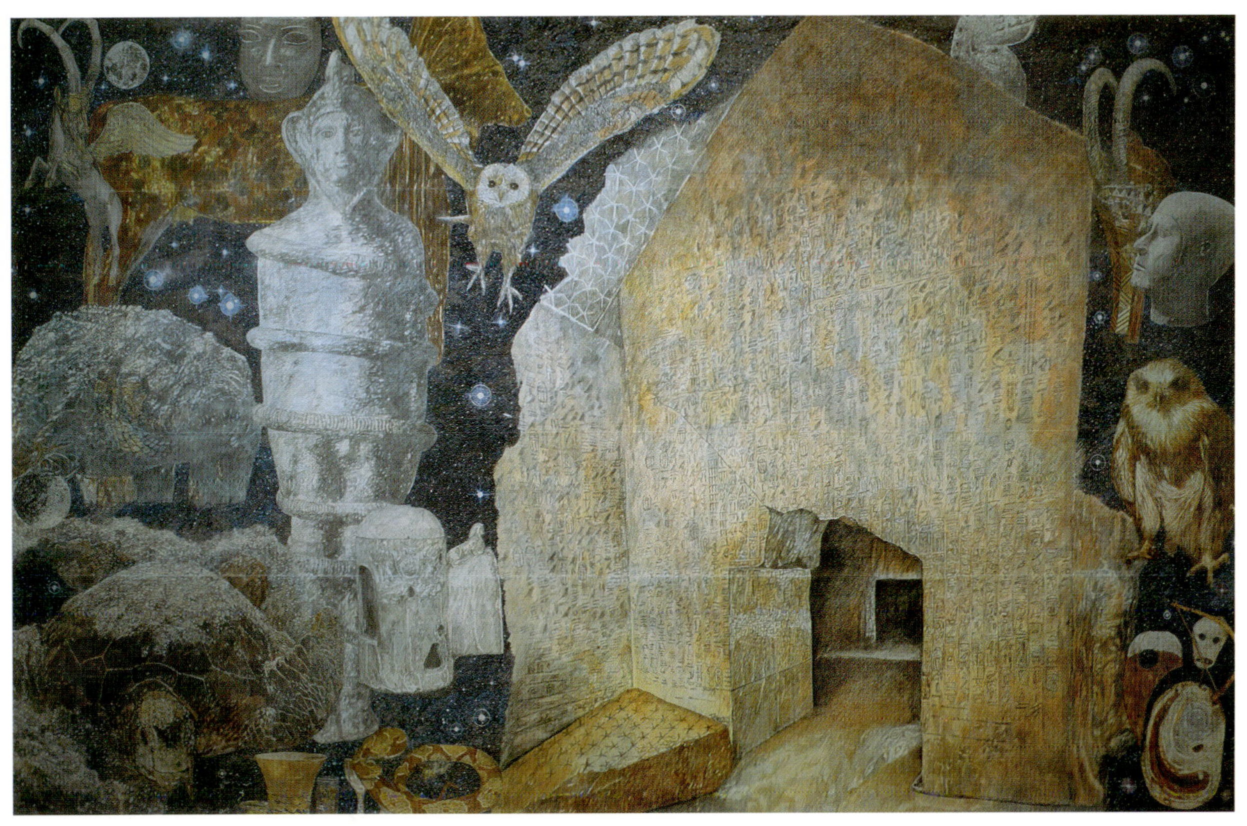

26. *Pyramid for Martin Hurson*, 1981

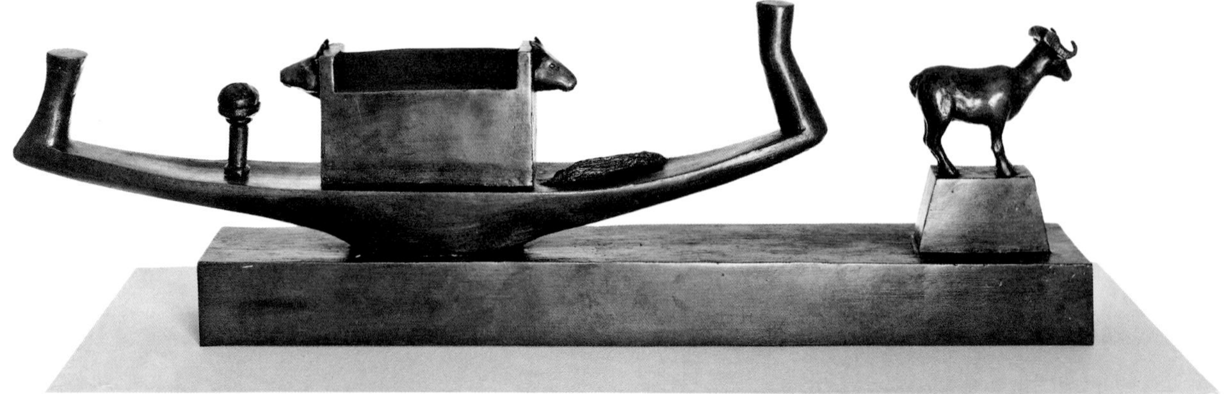

27. *Barque for Isis and Hathor*, 1984

strong personal symbol for the grave. Christ, like the king, also emerges as the spiritual man from the tomb, who first dies to be reborn.

Being Catholic, memento mori were for me familiar symbols of the Putrefactio process, the death that proceeds resurrection. The mummy has been in my dreams since childhood. "Life, verily, is naught but a kind of embalmed mummy, which preserves the mortal body from mortal worms," says Paracelsus. The decapitated head, caput mortuum (upper right), is often identified with the head of the black Osiris in alchemical literature. When the head is boiled, cooked in the alchemical process, it turns to gold. This image of scalping also appears in the *Visions of Zosimos*. Aion, the god of the inner sanctuaries, undergoes unendurable torments as part of the transformation process. The Putrefactio is linked to the Morificatio, a process which involves death, dismemberment, torment, and suffering. In a psy-

chological sense, insights are born from such individual suffering. The suffering on the cross becomes a symbol for an inner suffering that leads to new insights, a new life.

The stars in the background refer to the Nigredo, the darkest state of the alchemical Great Work. This stage of the work may be compared to the Dark Night of the Soul described by St. John of the Cross. From this Nigredo (the blackness), the new light (the stella matutina) emerges. Sparks of insight are born from the depths of defeat and darkness; a new adaptation can emerge.

The owl, the nocturnal bird of the spirit, flies through the work. The owl has similar meanings in both Egyptian and American Indian myths. The animal archetypes are also part of the process. In the *Egyptian Book of the Dead*, the sun god Ra sails his solar barque over the upper and lower firmaments. During the Hours of the Night, he assumes the forms of

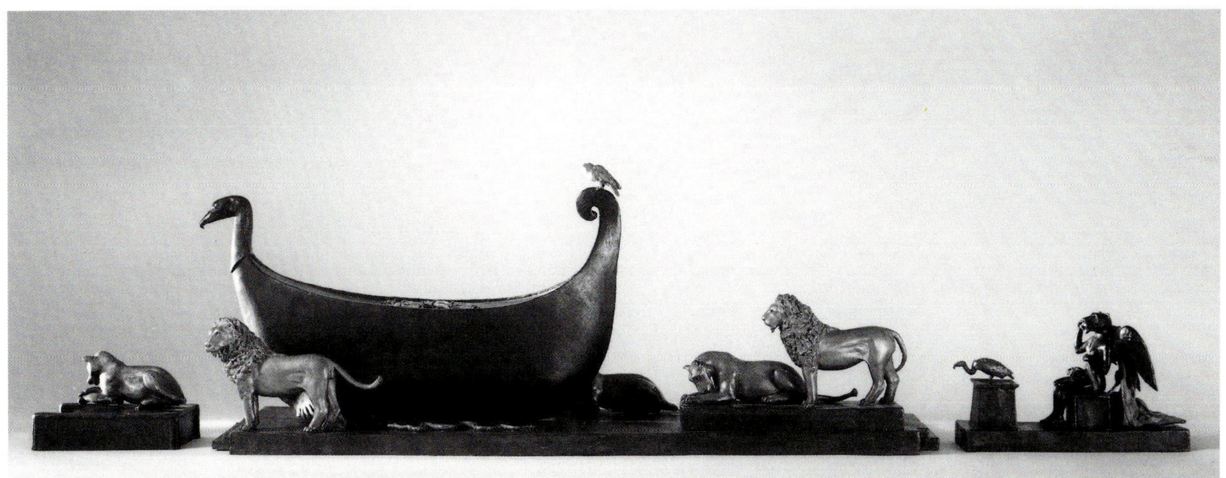

28. *Barque with Lion Goddess V*, 1985

the animal archetypes. In the dream life of the individual, the animals often represent instinctual parts of the process. The crocodile in some versions of the Osiris myth rescues the dismembered body parts of Osiris from the Nile so that they may be reconsituted by Isis.

The serpent, a chthonian deity, has multiple meanings. In alchemy, the serpent is often used to represent Mercurius, a personification of the unconscious. Alchemical texts often begin with the words "take a serpent . . ." The serpent is dual in nature and can represent not only this dual aspect of the unconscious, but also a kind of psychic/libidinal energy needed in the transformation process. The scope of serpent symbolism is too vast for this short essay. However, in the work shown, it is identified with "serpent power," the Kundalini. This energy travels through the centers of consciousness (the chackra).

The figure (left) is believed by most to be a representation of the Persian god Adad. Both Adad and the Persian goddess Atargatis, as well as Mithras and Aion, are often shown wrapped in a serpent, which bisects the body at the points of consciousness. This image clearly relates to the spiritual process described in the Kundalini. This image occurred in a dream I had about the interior of the pyramid. One is reminded of Nerval's *Voyage to the Orient* and his initiation inside the pyramid.

This mortification, this destruction, is difficult for the ego, yet is important in the life of the individual. This internal suffering brings the possibility for renewal. However difficult it is, it is necessary if one is to have new insights. As the Turba says, "Take the old black spirit and destroy and torture it with the bodies, until they are changed."

Ann McCoy, 1986

Stephen McKenna

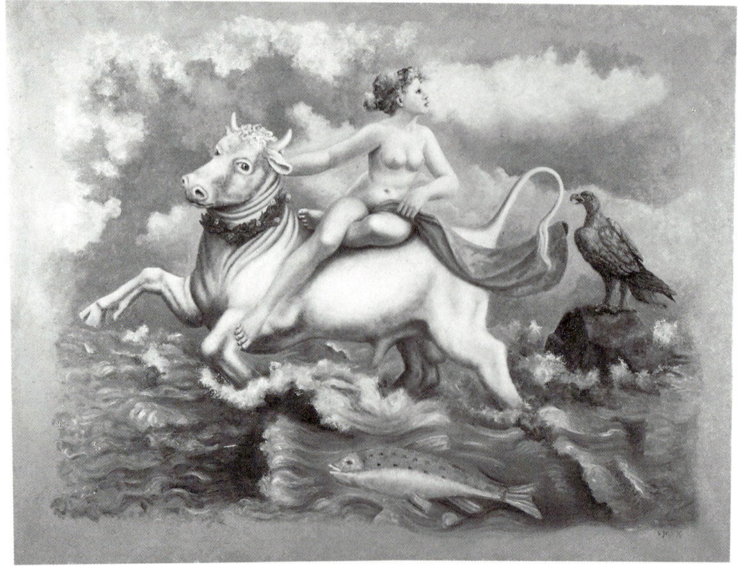

30. *Europe*, 1981

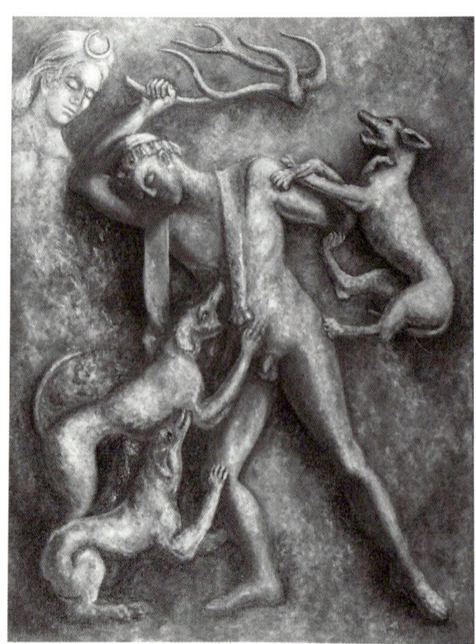

32. *Destruction of Acteon*, 1983

Given that our everyday experience of time is one-way, all events outside the ephemeral present are historical. Too great a concern with recent history, stretching back a generation or two, tends toward nostalgia. The urge to be up-to-date may be seen as a particular form of this, the currently fashionable being largely determined by a positive or negative reaction to the near past.

One of the attributes of paintings is a capacity for timelessness (in spite of the obvious physical changes to which they are subject), and the ability of art historians to date works precisely. This has less to do with matters of eternity than with the instinct of the painter to take an aerial view, rather than a linear perspective of culture. One should distinguish perennial subject matter, or content, from historical style. There is an equally fundamental difference between history and myth—the latter being a poetic, that is, a tangible emblem of human experience and desires.

A love of nature does not necessarily imply an interest in topography, just as the human figure is not indissolubly bound to its trappings, except in the special case of portraiture. All of this does not alter the fact that some of the best works of painting have been made in the field of portraiture, genre, and conversation pieces.

Stephen McKenna, 1986

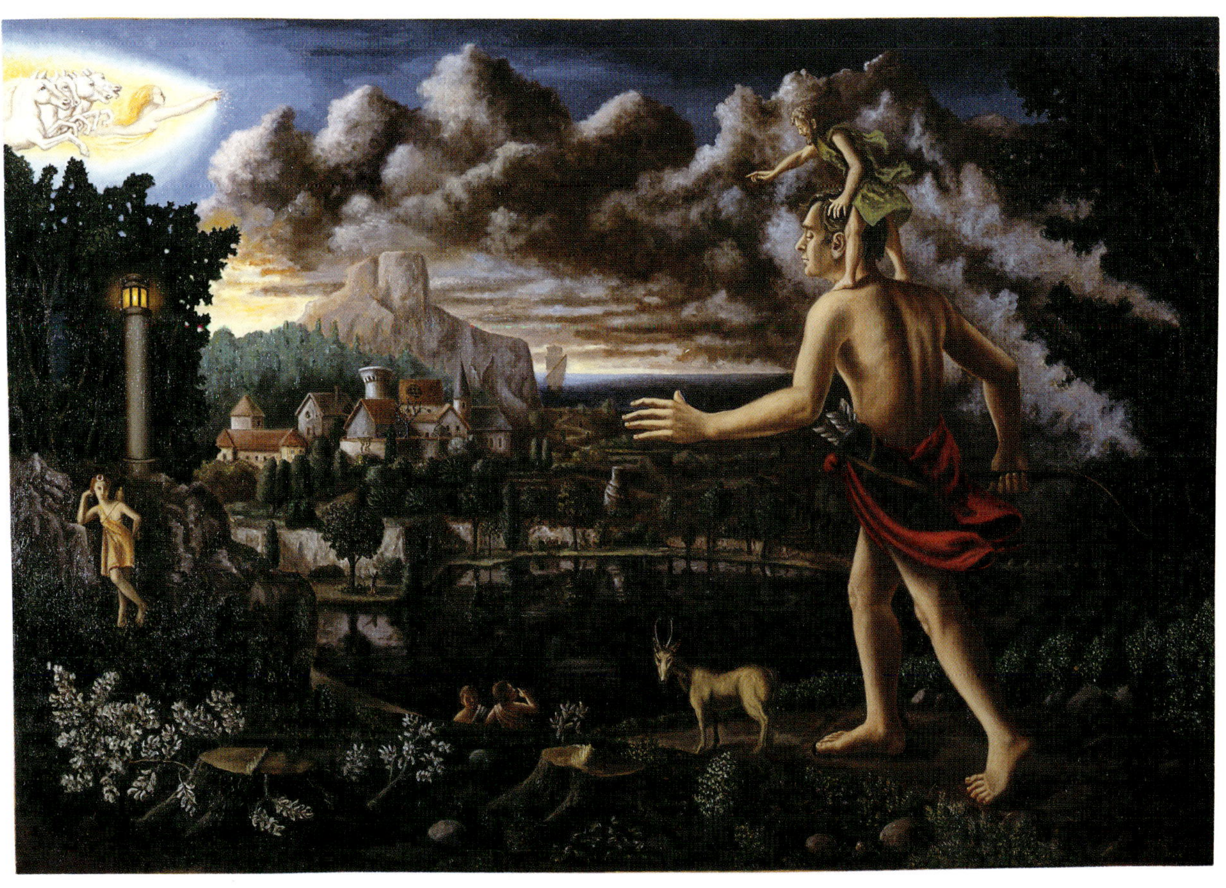

31.   *The Blind Orion with Eos and Artemis*, 1981

Odd Nerdrum

There are two key issues in art-making today: the presentness of past art and the status of the human figure in art. These issues are closely related: the use of the figure is central to the interest in allegorical iconography which is an important dimension of the various stylistic revivals that are prevalent today. With this revived interest in the figure's meaning comes a new curiosity about its aesthetic potential. However, the figure still seems to be regarded cautiously: it is looked at from the outside, as an intriguing visual novelty with a familiar symbolic value. It is not rethought subjectively, or rather, the subjective understanding of it tends to take conventional modernist form. By being presented as "agitated," to use the fashionable term, it is made "superficially" subjective. That is, its fresh expressionistic skin renews its modernist value as a symbol of universal anxiety. But this anxiety has become a cliché, like the expressionist language that bespeaks it. There is theatrical opportunism in the "reagitation" of the figure.

The problem is: how to restore a sense of the full psychic reality of the figure—more complex and full than the one-dimensionalizing anxiety that is supposed to be the linchpin of human constitution—and convey it through the subtle reality of the lived body. Odd Nerdrum shows us how: by returning to a traditional sense of the inherent value of the body and using it as a language to convey a sense of the psychic state of the person. Today it is the traditional language of bodily presence the Old Masters used to articulate their sense of the significance of human existence that seems fresh, fundamental—that no longer seems stereotyped. It has become the context in which to grow artistically, rather than the modernist language which, in being created, and in becoming an end in itself, has eliminated many of the humanistic issues that art once dealt with as a matter of course—has made them seem irrelevant to "authentic" art, reduced them to the status of the "merely literary." Not that these issues are valid today simply because they were valid yesterday. And not that the language of the Old Masters seems authentic again (and underused) simply because modernist language no longer seems authentic (and overused). Rather, the necessity

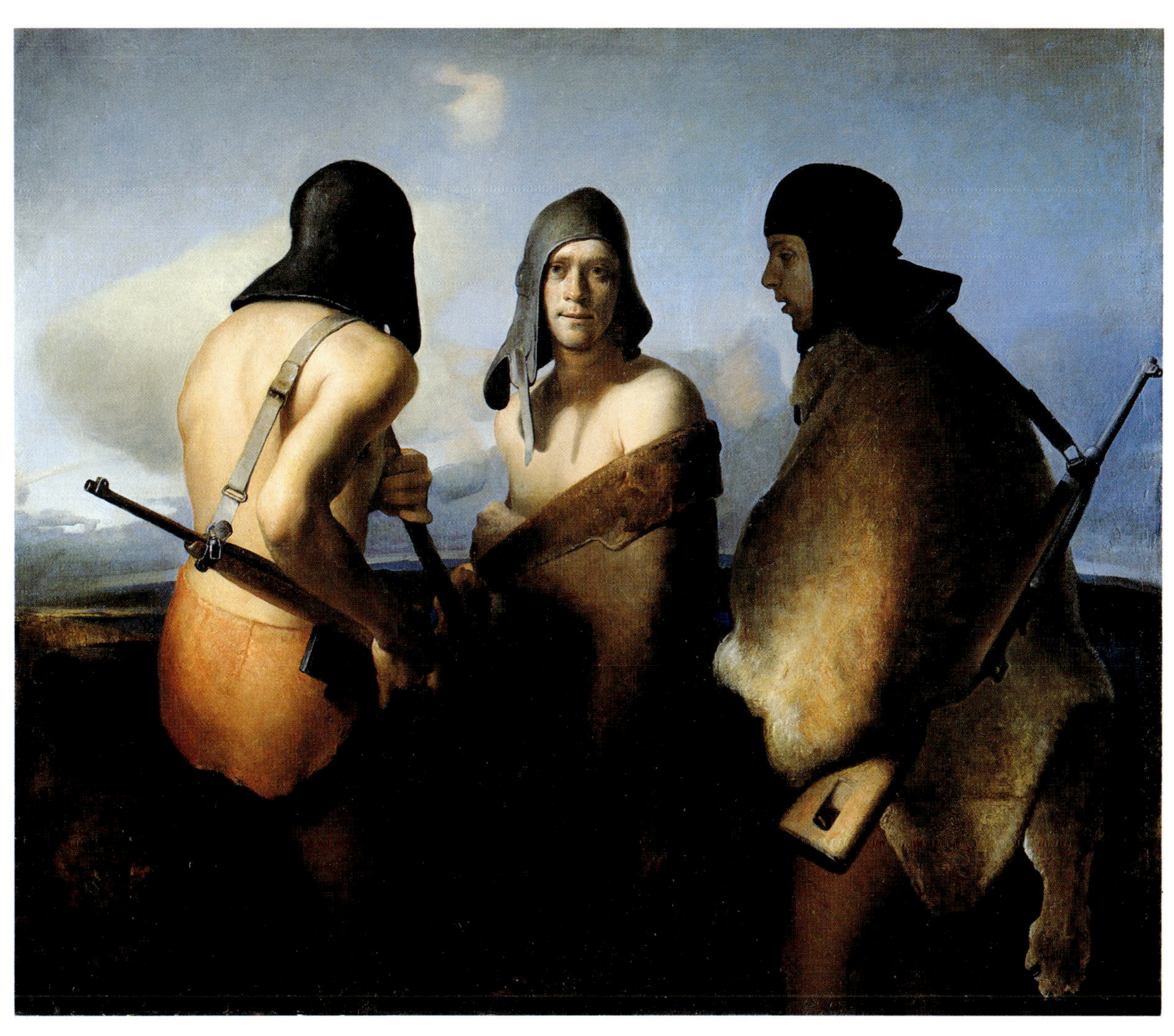

35. *The Water Protectors*, 1985

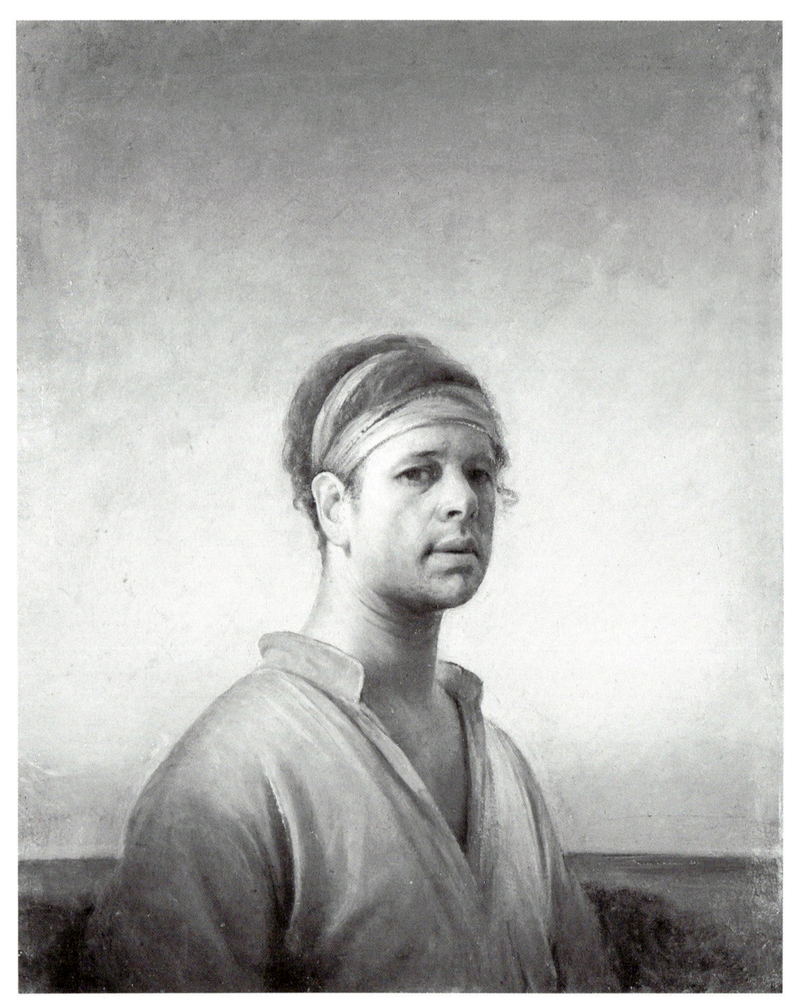

34. *Man with a Headband*, 1984

for a renewal of interest in humanistic issues
and a humanistic language of art have become
crucial in the modern world, which has not suf-
ficiently focused upon the central, most
serious human issue of our time: whether man
will survive his own science and technology—
his own modernity. Nerdrum's art deals
directly with this pre- and post-apocalyptic
issue by allegorically articulating the solitude
of the human figure as a symbol of its survival
against all odds—a survival not absolutely
assured, but still proclaimed as possible.

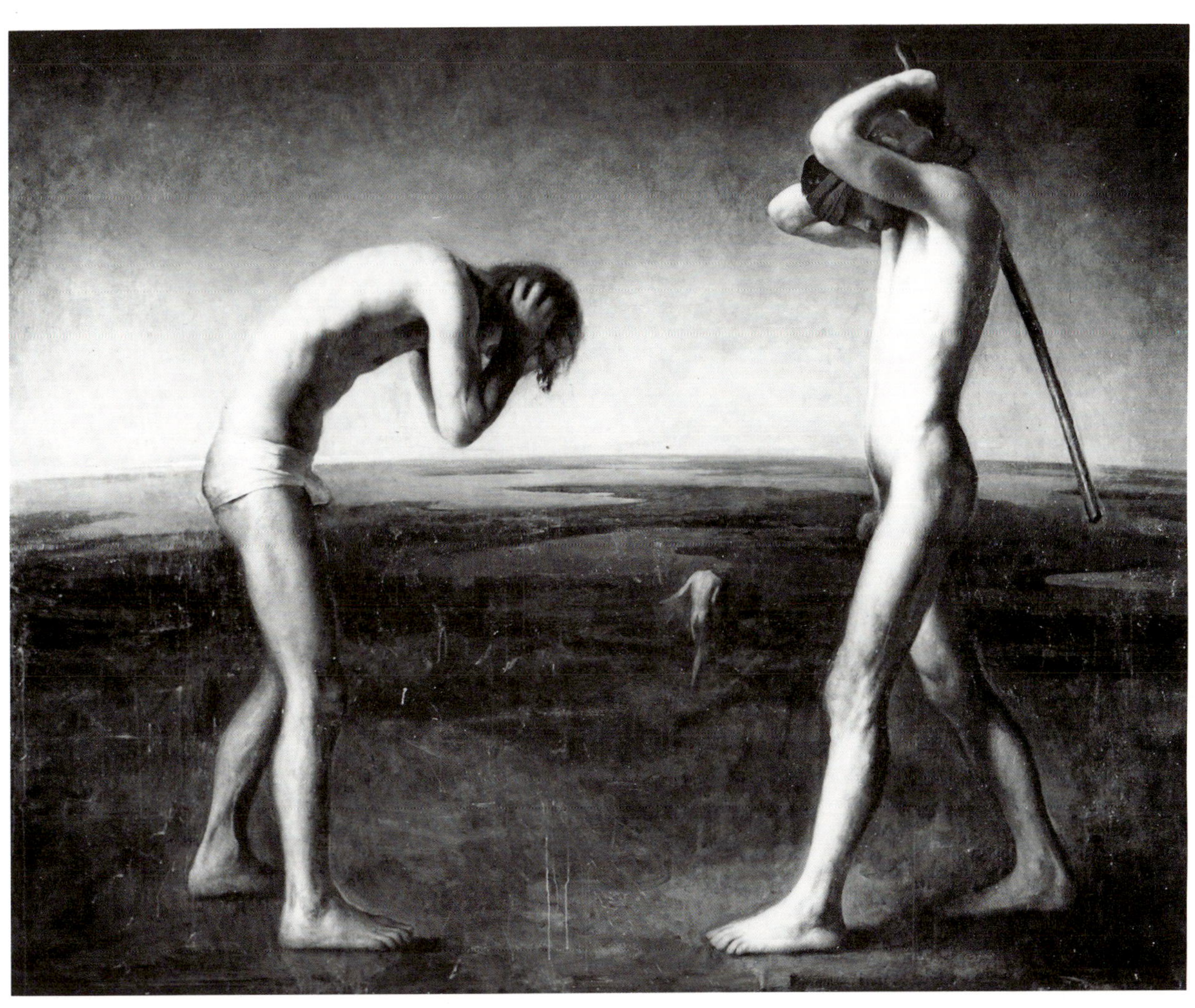

33. *Iron Law*, 1983–84

Giulio Paolini

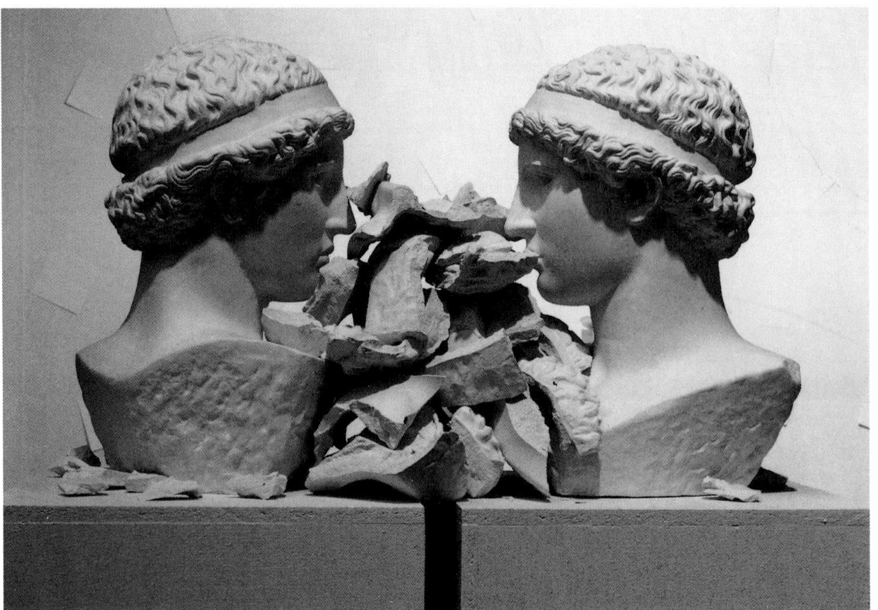

37.   *L'altra figura*, 1983

While no drawing exists without a line, the line "moves" as in a chess game. Without the complement of an object, that is, without becoming in time, it appears where it is supposed to appear. Thus, drawing is somewhat similar to the orthographic wonder of a capital initial in a line of poetry: the immobile running of streams of water when the thaw begins; petals and leaves abandoned to the wind in a sudden gust; the procedure of the dictated outlines of mountains and nations.

All precarious and precious motives as brought to light by the hand of the archeologist who diligently attends to the traces prearranged by time.

Again, what is a drawing? The so rare and so obvious combination of all the things that are marvellously in their places: bird's-eye view or a vision with closed eyes; the smile displayed by the acrobat in the most delicate moment of his exercise; the ancient profile of ruins, which seem to be constituting themselves and remaining at the same time; the golden reflection of the curtain fringes, sealing the expectation of an event...

Giulio Paolini, 1983

Excerpt from P.S. 1, The Institute for Art and Urban Resources, New York, and Umberto Allemandi & C., *The Knot: Arte Povera at P.S. 1* (1985), by Germano Celant. Used by permission.

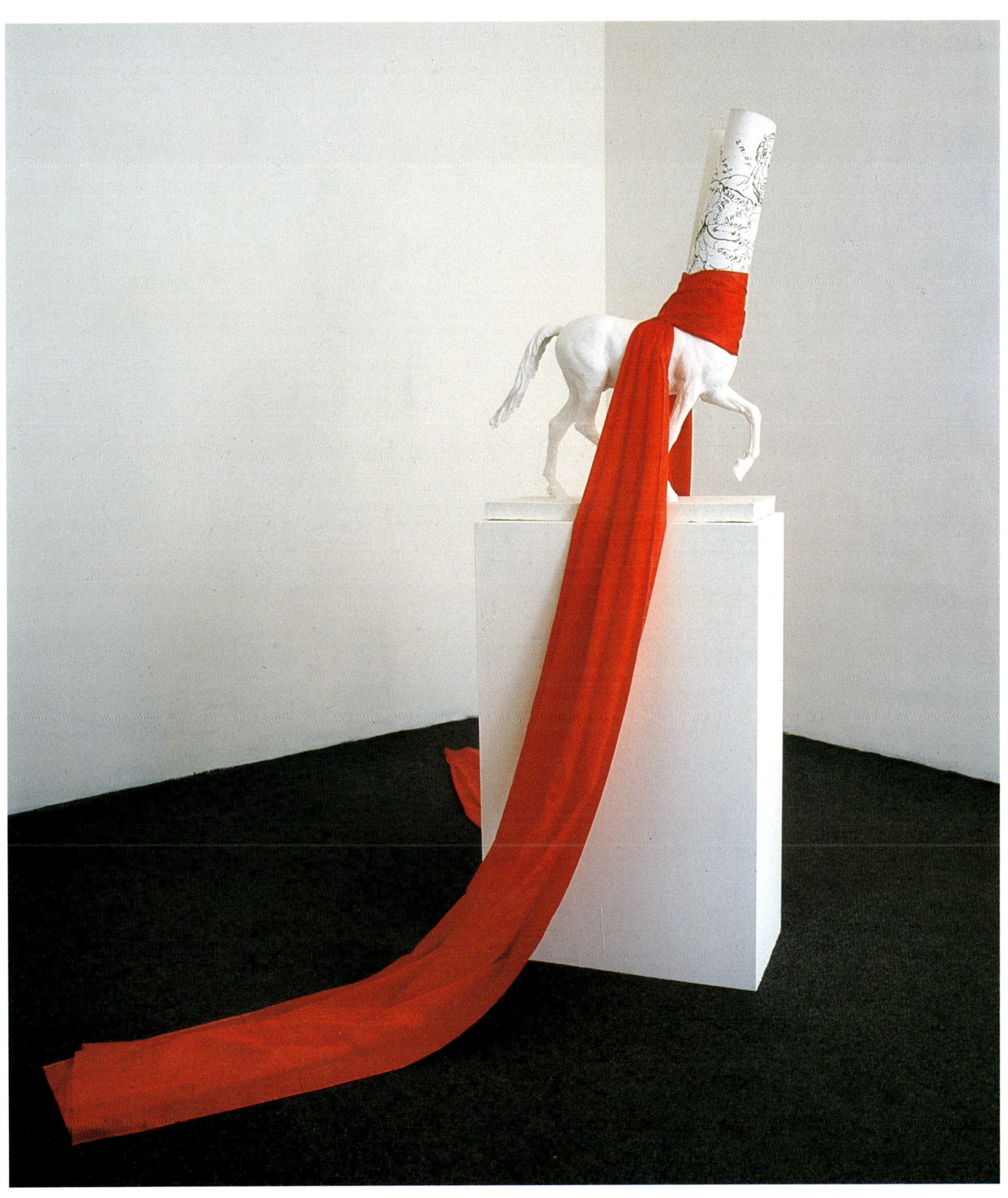

36.   *Nesso (Nessus)*, 1977

Earl Staley

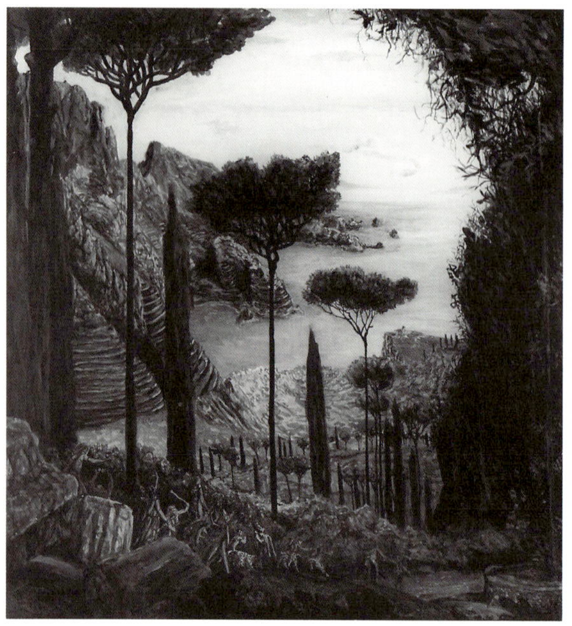

38.   *Triumph of Bacchus II*, 1982

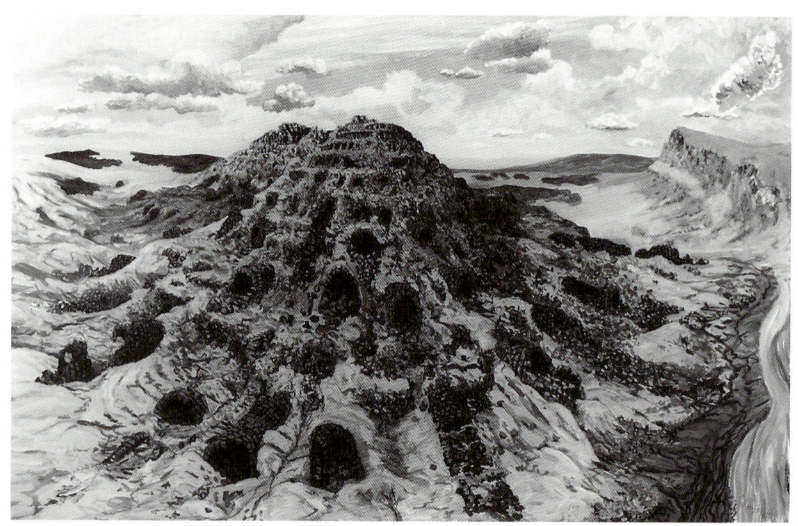

40.   *Tower of Babel*, 1985

I want my pictures to be intellectually and visu-
ally stimulating and I want them to tell interest-
ing stories.

I use universal historical imagery—classic,
religious, or popular—because it best explains
contemporary life.

I paint because it gives me pleasure.

Earl Staley, 1986

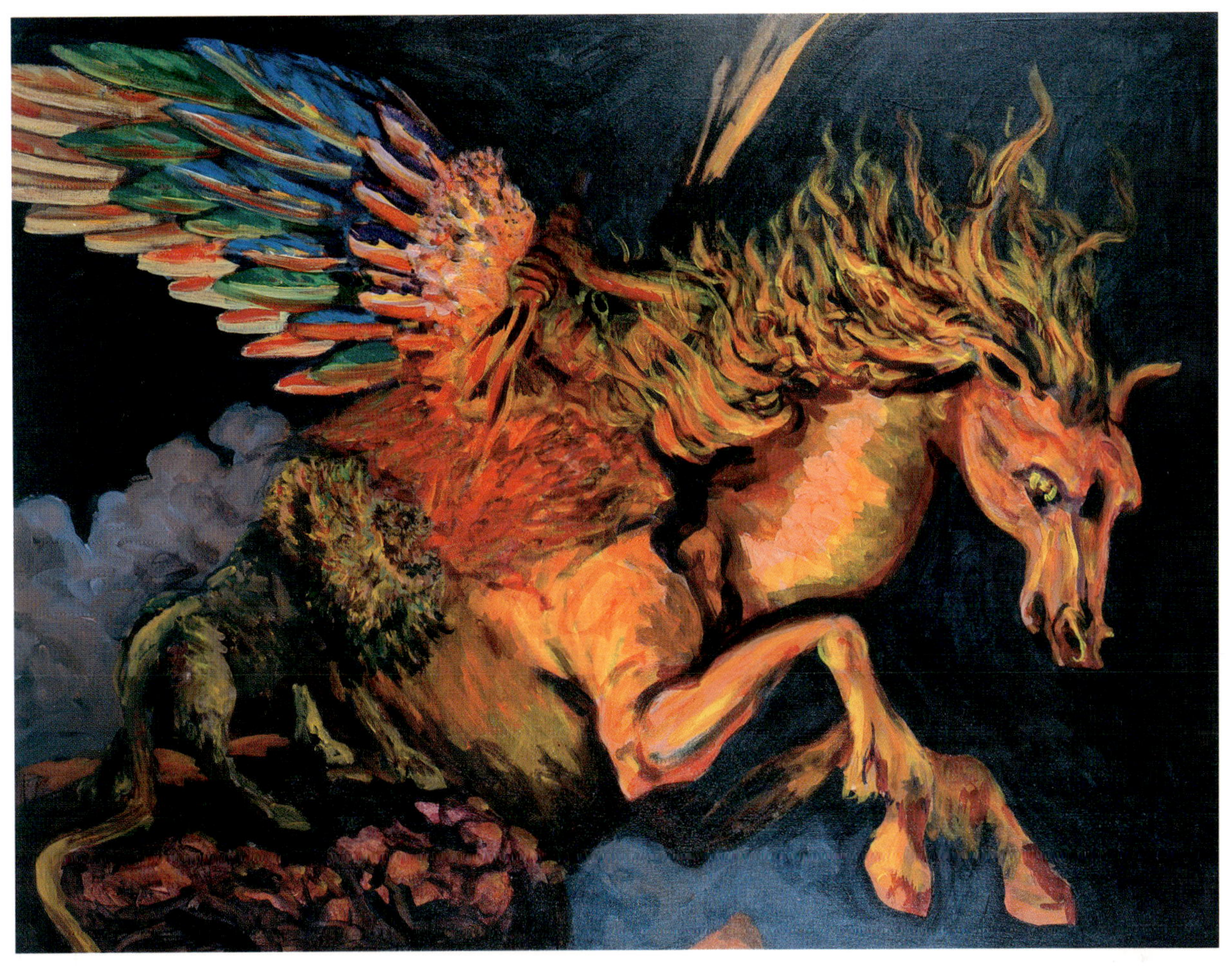

39. *Bellerophon IV*, 1984

M. Louise Stanley

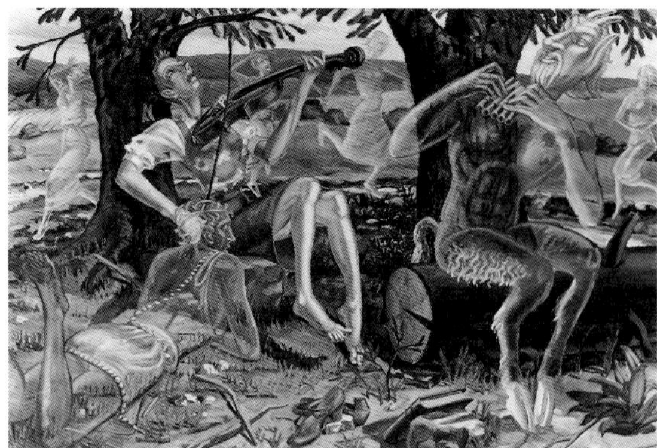

42.   *Symphonica Allegoriosa*, 1985

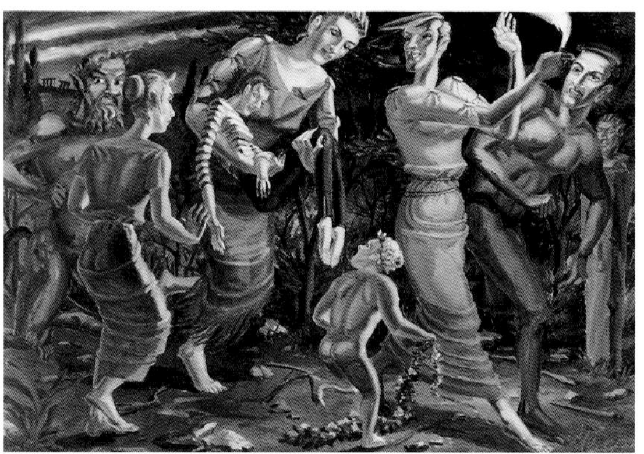

41.   *Birth of an Idea*, 1985

I began using classical references because I wished to monumentalize the trivial aspects of my subject matter: male-female relationships and my own experiences. Along with humor, these references camouflage the more personal content, entertain me, and throw another contradiction onto the pile.

As a child I rode my bike to the Huntington Library every weekend. I devoured the paintings and tapestries, then moved to the gardens to act out the dramas I had just seen. Much of the collection (eighteenth- and nineteenth-century British) was portraiture based on classical themes. I was fascinated by the corniness of paintings such as of Mrs. Siddons acting as a goddess in white chiffon.

If Reynolds and Gainsborough can get away with it, why not me?

My paintings are triggered by an experience or place. As I paint, I embellish the memory by re-staging the scene. *Symphonica Allegoriosa* is about fantasy. In this case, it's a much-needed vacation by an idyllic stream, peopled with friends conjured up to keep me company during long hours in my studio.

The *Pompeian Villa* is a prop, an elaborate frame for *Pygmaliana*. It is also a place for me to enter and become my own self-portrait.

The Romans collected red-and-black Athenian vases and I have always wanted one of my own, so I included papier-mâché copies. I made a statue of Hermes, the god of fertility, travel, and commerce. As I was finishing, I discovered a book by Eva Keuls, *The Reign of the Phallus*, which attempts to solve the mystery of "the Mutilation of the Herm," which occurred in 400 B.C. in Athens. My solution to the crime, *Athena, Multilating a Herm: An Historical Re-enactment*, came out of my anger at this discovery: as a woman, had I lived in ancient Greece my fantasies would never have been realized.

This has dampened my interest in the Greeks, but not my fantasies.

M. Louise Stanley, 1986

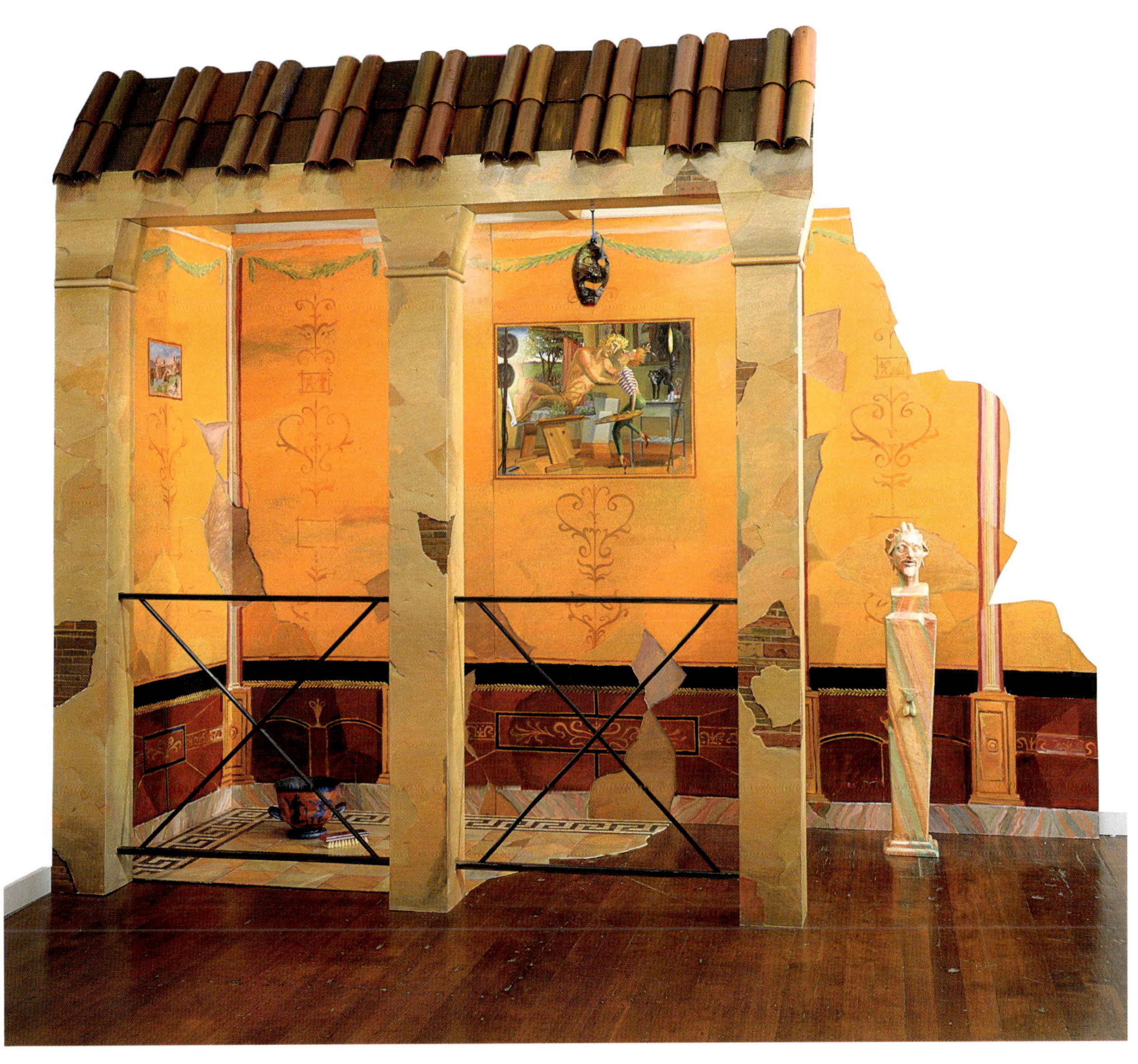

43. *Pompeian Villa*, 1985-86

Michelle Stuart

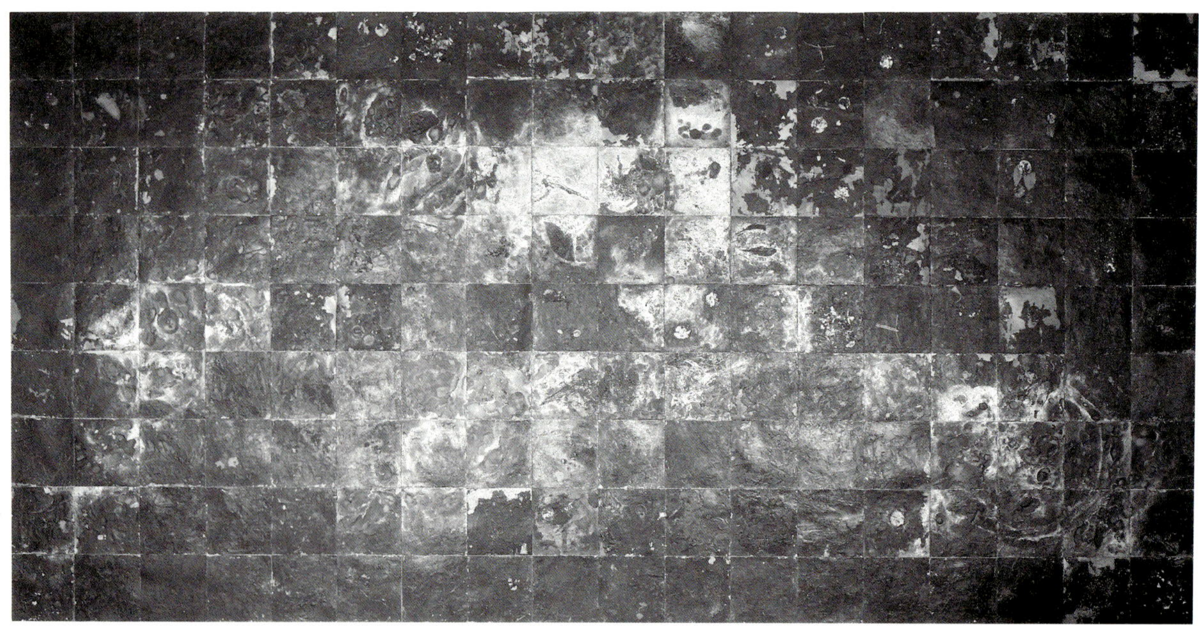

46.   *In the Beginning . : . Yan-Na*, 1984

Structures and patterns of thought vary between cultures and times. To understand oneself and the place and time within which one lives (dreams) one must collaborate with memory. Memory is All Time. The referential materials in my work—earth, shards, fossils, plants—exist to explore the depths of those structures and patterns. With them I try to make the invisible passages of time visible, to extract insight from sight, and to exhume from my memory a consciousness of cor-respondences.

Michelle Stuart, 1986

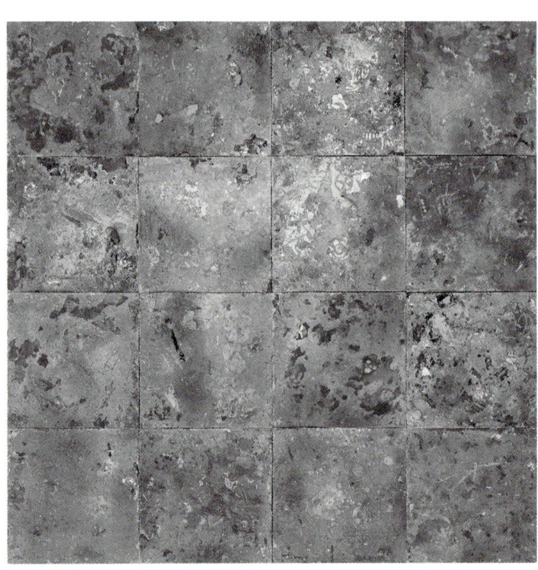

47.   *Anoka (Minnesota)*, 1985

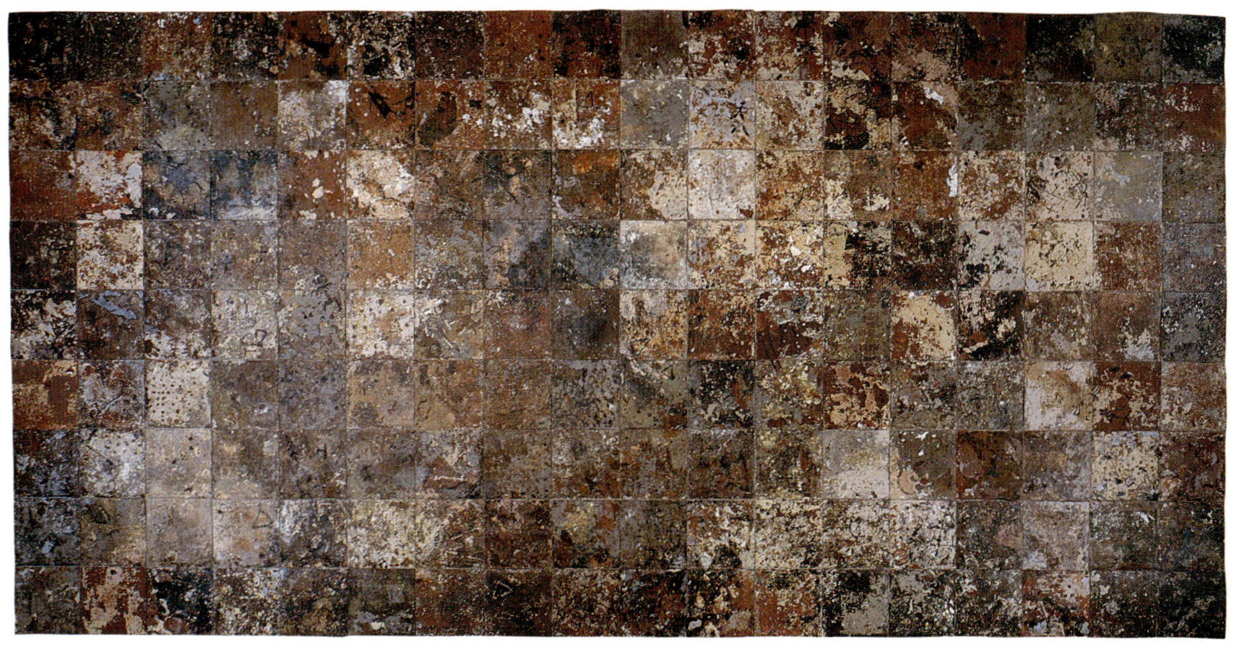

48.   *Red . . . Earth. Dream Wall of the Big House*, 1985–86

Mark Tansey

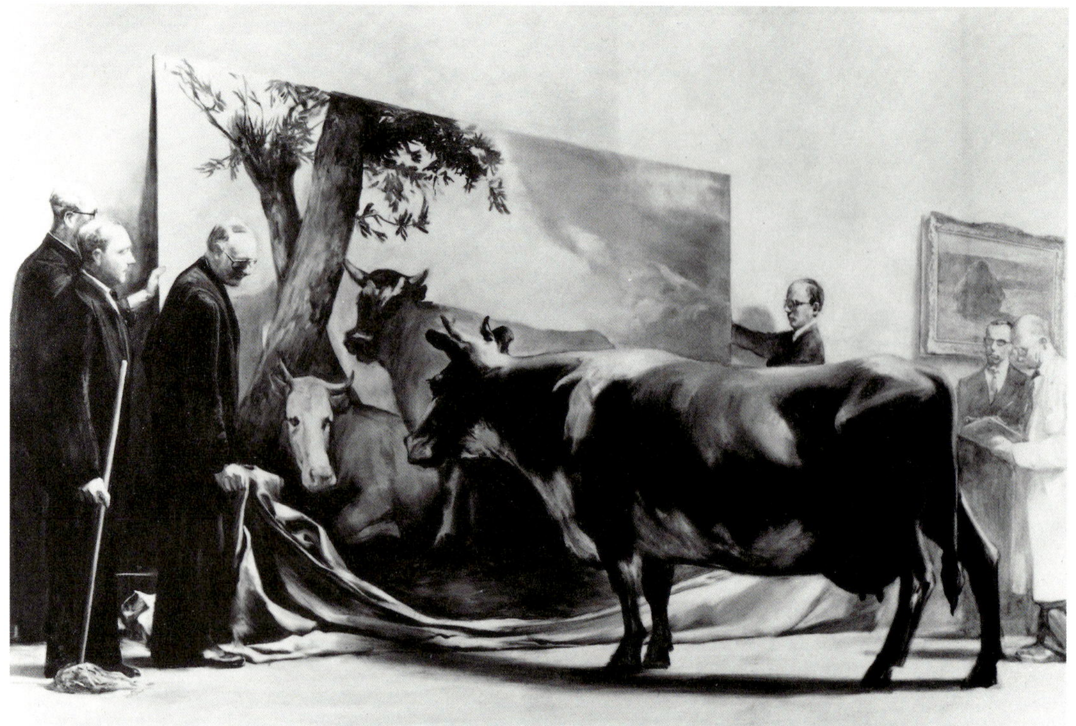

49.   *The Innocent Eye Test*, 1981

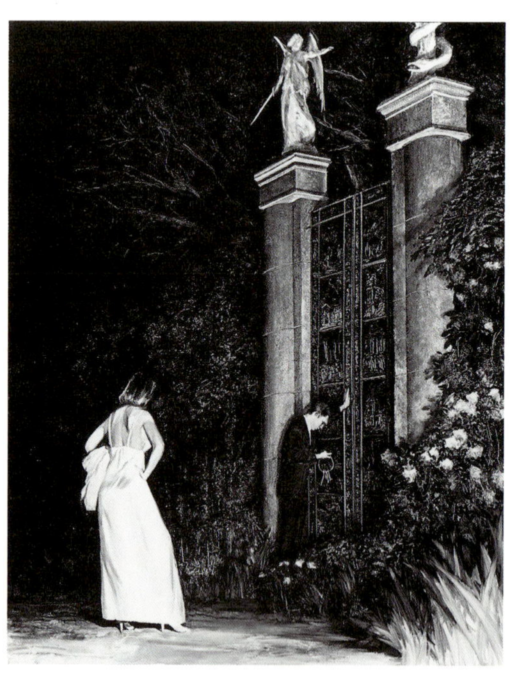

50.   *The Key*, 1984

A painted picture is a vehicle. One can either
sit in the driveway and take it apart or one can
get in it and go somewhere.

Mark Tansey, 1986

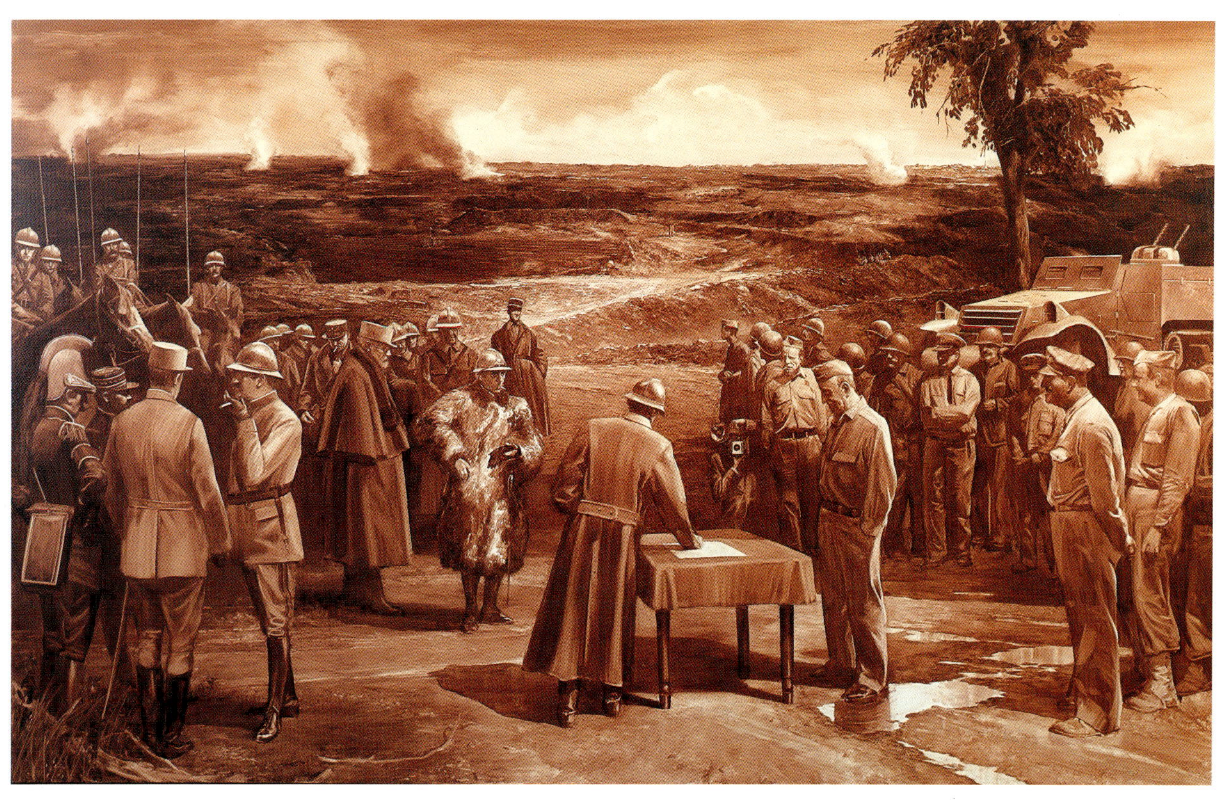

51.   *Triumph of the New York School*, 1984

Hermann Albert

1. *Pferd und Akt am Meer (Der Abend)*, 1984
tempera on canvas
98 x 80″ (248.9 x 203.2)
Byron Meyer, San Francisco

2. *The Sculptor*, 1985
tempera on canvas
59 x 51″ (149.9 x 129.5)
Courtesy Rena Bransten Gallery, San Francisco

Edward Allington

3. *Decorative Fragments*, 1986
ink and emulsion on paper
21 x 29″ (53.3 x 73.7)
Courtesy Diane Brown Gallery, New York

4. *The Past Recycled: Metropolitan Egypt*, 1986
plaster casts and stuccoed wood
64 x 34 ½ x 66″ (162.6 x 87.6 x 167.6)
Martin Sklar, New York

5. *Three and Four Steps*, 1986
plaster and stuccoed wood
58 x 79 x 108″ (147.3 x 200.7 x 271.8)
Courtesy Diane Brown Gallery, New York

6. *With Acanthus Support*, 1986
plaster casts and stuccoed wood
44 x 21 ½ x 21 ½″ (111.8 x 54.6 x 54.6)
Courtesy Diane Brown Gallery, New York

Siah Armajani

7. *Dictionary for Building: Fireplace Mantle with Windows*, 1982–83
painted wood and mirror
84 x 46 ½ x 27 ½″ (213.4 x 118.1 x 69.8)
Lent by the artist; courtesy Max Protetch Gallery, New York

8. *Dictionary for Building: Closet Under Landing*, 1985
painted wood, stain, and mirror
110 x 46 ½ x 104″ (278.4 x 118.1 x 264.2)
Lent by the artist; courtesy Max Protetch Gallery, New York

Roger Brown

9. *Adam and Eve (Expulsion from the Garden)*, 1982
oil on canvas
48 x 72″ (121.9 x 182.9)
Virginia Museum of Fine Arts, Richmond, gift of Sydney and Frances Lewis 85.366

10. *Galvanized Temple*, 1985
galvanized metal and aluminum
40 x 38 ¼ x 53 ¾″ (101.6 x 97.2 x 136.5)
Courtesy Phyllis Kind Gallery, New York

Harry Fritzius

11. *Michelangelo after the Sistine Chapel No. 1*, 1985
oil on canvas
85 x 90″ (215.9 x 228.6)
Donald J. Putterman and Adrienne Sherman, San Francisco

12. *Study after Rubens*, 1985
oil on canvas
75 x 90″ (190.5 x 228.6)
John and Marcia Bachner, Great Falls, Virginia

13. *Laocoön after El Greco*, 1986
81 x 116″ (205.7 x 294.6)
oil on canvas
Courtesy Bruce Velick Gallery, San Francisco

Douglas Higgins

14. *Prometheus*, 1984
acrylic, oil, pencil, oil crayon, and collage on linen
58 x 46³⁄₁₆″ (147.3 x 117.3)
Mr. and Mrs. Jerome Siegel, Mamaroneck, New York

15. *Rams of Asarkaya*, 1985
acrylic, oil, oil crayon and pencil on linen
46 ⅝ x 72 ½″ (118.4 x 184.1)
Courtesy Ruth Siegel Ltd, New York, and Janet Steinberg Gallery, San Francisco

16. *Melancholia (after Dürer)*, 1986
acrylic, oil, modelling paste, marble dust, pencil, colored pencil, and oil crayon on canvas
74 x 85 ½″ (188 x 217.2)
Courtesy Ruth Siegel Ltd, New York, and Janet Steinberg Gallery, San Francisco

David Hollowell

17. *La Galleria*, 1985
oil and wax on masonite
120 x 240″ (303.8 x 607.6)
Courtesy Jane Haslem Gallery, Washington, D.C.

Komar and Melamid

18. *Nostalgic View of the Kremlin from Manhattan*, 1981–82
oil on canvas
72 x 87″ (182.9 x 221)
Robert and Maryse Boxer, London; courtesy Ronald Feldman Fine Arts Inc., New York

19. *Venus of Milo*, 1983
oil on canvas
72 x 48″ (182.9 x 121.9)
Courtesy Ronald Feldman Fine Arts Inc., New York

20. *When I Was a Child Matzoh Reminded Me of a Braille Book*, 1984–85
mixed media
54 ¼ x 92 x 3 ½″ (137.8 x 233.7 x 8.9)
Courtesy Ronald Feldman Fine Arts Inc., New York

Christopher Le Brun

21. *Prow*, 1983
oil on canvas
102 x 102″ (258.1 x 258.1)
PaineWebber Group Inc.
Collection, New York

22. *Wreath*, 1983
oil on canvas
65 ½ x 73″ (166.4 x 185.4)
Anne and William J. Hokin
Collection, Chicago

Carlo Maria Mariani

23. *La Mano Ubbidisce all'Intelletto
(The Hand Submits to the Intellect)*, 1983
oil on canvas
78 ½ x 69″ (199.4 x 175.3)
Anne and William J. Hokin
Collection, Chicago

24. *Ecco sei tu, Eletto*, 1983
pencil and gouache on paper
86 ½ x 70 ¾ ″ (219.7 x 179.7)
Courtesy Sperone Westwater,
New York

25. *Guardarsi in uno specchio celeste
(Looking into a Celestial Mirror)*,
1984
oil on canvas
93 ⅜ x 78 ¾ ″ (237.2 x 200)
Courtesy Sperone Westwater,
New York

Ann McCoy

26. *Pyramid for Martin Hurson*,
1981
pencil and colored pencil on
paper mounted on canvas
107 ⅞ x 167 ½ ″ (272.6 x 425.4)
Hirshhorn Museum and
Sculpture Garden, Smith-
sonian Institution, partial gift
of Mrs. Bettina Bancroft and
Museum Purchase, 1982

27. *Barque for Isis and Hathor*, 1984
cast bronze
12 x 40 ½ x 4 ¾ ″ (30.5 x 102.9
x 12.1)
BankAmerica Corporation
Art Collection, San Francisco

28. *Barque with Lion Goddess V*,
1985
cast bronze
42 x 10 x 16 ½ ″; 9 x 5 ¼ x 5″;
12 ½ x 3 ¾ x 6″ (106.7 x 25.4 x
41.2; 22.9 x 13.3 x 12.7; 31.7 x
9.5 x 15.2)
Mr. and Mrs. Sidney Singer

29. *Barque with Lion Goddess VI*,
1985
cast and painted bronze
3 ¾ x 12 ¾ x 4 ½ ″ (9.5 x 32.4
x 11.4)
Mr. and Mrs. Richard F.
Polich

Stephen McKenna

30. *Europe*, 1981
oil on canvas
60 x 80″ (152.4 x 203.2)
Courtesy Sander Gallery,
New York

31. *The Blind Orion with Eos and
Artemis*, 1981
oil on canvas
59 x 84″ (149.9 x 213.4)
Wilhelm Shurman; courtesy
Sander Gallery, New York

32. *Destruction of Acteon*, 1983
oil on canvas
79 x 59″ (200.7 x 149.9)
Courtesy Sander Gallery,
New York

Odd Nerdrum

33. *Iron Law*, 1983–84
oil on canvas
82 x 114″ (208.3 x 288.6)
Courtesy Martina Hamilton
Gallery, New York

34. *Man with a Headband*, 1984
oil on canvas
35 x 29″ (88.9 x 73.7)
Courtesy Martina Hamilton
Gallery, New York

35. *The Water Protectors*, 1985
oil on canvas
60 x 72″ (152.4 x 182.9)
Courtesy Martina Hamilton
Gallery, New York

Giulio Paolini

36. *Nesso (Nessus)*, 1977
plaster with acrylic,
lithograph, and synthetic
fabric
74 ½ x 73 ½ x 16 ⅛ ″ (189.2
x 186.7 x 41)
San Francisco Museum of
Modern Art, Mrs. Paul L.
Wattis Fund Purchase 86.5

37. *L'altra figura*, 1983
plaster with wood base
47 ¼ x 15 ¾ x 15 ¾ ″ (120
x 40 x 40)
Courtesy Marian Goodman
Gallery, New York

Earl Staley

38. *Triumph of Bacchus II*, 1982
acrylic on canvas
64 x 60″ (162.6 x 152.4)
Mrs. Earl Staley, Houston;
courtesy Texas Gallery,
Houston

39. *Bellerophon IV*, 1984
acrylic on canvas
47 ¼ x 63″ (120 x 160)
Edward R. Downe, Jr.

40. *Tower of Babel*, 1985
acrylic on canvas
60 x 96″ (152.4 x 243.8)
Courtesy Texas Gallery,
Houston

M. Louise Stanley

41. *Birth of an Idea*, 1985
oil on canvas
36 x 52″ (91.4 x 132.1)
Lent by the artist; courtesy
Rena Bransten Gallery, San
Francisco

42. *Symphonica Allegoriosa*, 1985
oil on canvas
36 x 54″ (91.4 x 137.2)
Lent by the artist; courtesy
Rena Bransten Gallery, San
Francisco

43. *Pompeian Villa*, 1985–86
acrylic on masonite, paper
mache
114 x 144 x 54″ (288.6 x 364.8
x 137.2)
Lent by the artist; courtesy
Rena Bransten Gallery, San
Francisco

Pat Steir

44. *The Brueghel Series (A Vanitas
of Style)—Monochrome: 2nd
Version*, 1982–85
oil on canvas
110 x 84″ (278.4 x 213.4)
Agnes Gund,
New York

45. *The Wave after Courbet (Eye of
the Storm)*, 1986
oil on linen
84 x 168″ (213.4 x 426.7)
Lent by the artist; courtesy
Michael Klein Inc., New York,
and Richard Kuhlenschmidt
Gallery, Los Angeles

Michelle Stuart

46. *In the Beginning... Yan-Na*,
1984
earth, bones, shells, plants,
encaustic, and pigment on
canvas-mounted rag paper
99 x 198″ (251.5 x 501.9)
Lent by the artist; courtesy
Max Protetch Gallery,
New York

47. *Anoka (Minnesota)*, 1985
earth, fossils from the banks
of the Mississippi River,
shells, plants, encaustic,
archaeological shards from
Anoka County, Minnesota,
and pigment on canvas-
mounted rag paper
44 x 44″ (111.8 x 111.8)
Lent by the artist; courtesy
Max Protetch Gallery,
New York

48. *Red... Earth. Dream Wall of the
Big House*, 1985–86
earth from New Mexico and
encaustic on canvas-mounted
rag paper
99 x 198″ (251.5 x 501.9)
Lent by the artist; courtesy
Max Protetch Gallery,
New York

Mark Tansey

49. *The Innocent Eye Test*, 1981
oil on canvas
78 x 120″ (198.1 x 304.8)
The Metropolitan Museum of
Art, New York, extended loan
and promised gift of Charles
Cowles

50. *The Key*, 1984
oil on canvas
60 x 48″ (152.4 x 121.9)
John Berggruen, San
Francisco

51. *Triumph of the New York School*,
1984
oil on canvas
74 x 120″ (188 x 303.8)
Whitney Museum of Ameri-
can Art, New York, promised
gift of Robert M. and Nancy
L. Kaye P.5.84

Artists' Biographies and Bibliographies

Hermann Albert

Born in 1937 in Ansbach/Mittelfranken, Federal Republic of Germany. Selected one-person exhibitions include Grossgorcshen 35, Berlin, 1967; Schubert Gallery, Milan, and L'Indiano Gallery, Florence, 1972; Der Spiegel Gallery, Cologne, 1977; Bucholz Gallery, Munich, 1978; Schloss Charlottenburg, Berlin, 1981 (cat.); Hermeyer Gallery, Munich, 1982; Raab Gallery, Berlin, and Sander Gallery, New York, 1985 (cat.); Rena Bransten Gallery, San Francisco, 1986. Selected group exhibitions include *Principle Realism*, Academy of Art, Berlin, 1973; *14 x 14*, Baden-Baden Kunsthalle, Federal Republic of Germany, 1974; *First Berlin Biennale*, Museum of Modern Art, Rio de Janeiro, 1975; *10 German Artists*, Louisiana Museum, Copenhagen, 1976; *International Realism Today*, Kunstverein, Hamburg, 1979; *Forms of Realism Today*, Poland and Canada, 1980; *Contemporary German Artists*, Moscow and Leningrad, 1982. Currently lives and works in Ribbesbuttel, Federal Republic of Germany, and Ronzano, Italy.

Selected publications include Robert Pincus-Witten, "Entires: Analytical Cubism," *Arts Magazine*, January 1985; Angela Vettese, "Europe and America: Two Aspects of the New Surreal," *Flash Art*, April/May 1985; Susanna Gaertner, "The Berlin Story," *Art and Auction*, May 1985; Bernhard Schulz, "Return of Things," *Flash Art*, May/June 1986.

Edward Allington

Born in 1951 in Troutbeck Bridge, Westmorland, England. Selected one-person exhibitions include Spacex Gallery, Exeter, England, 1981; Exe Gallery, Exeter, England, 1982; I.C.A., London, 1983 (cat.); Lisson Gallery, London, and Midland Group, Nottingham, England, 1984 (cat.); Riverside Studios, London (cat.), Lisson Gallery, London, (cat.), and Northern Centre for Contemporary Art, Sunderland, England, 1985 (cat.); Abbot Hall Gallery, Kendal, England, and Diane Brown Gallery, New York, 1986. Selected group exhibitions include *Summer Show*, Serpentine Gallery, London, 1976; *British Drawing*, Fruitmarket Gallery, London, and *Hayward Annual 1982*, Hayward Gallery, London, 1982; *Sculptors Drawings*, Air Gallery, London, *The Sculpture Show*, Hayward Gallery, London (cat.), *Beelden 83*, Rotterdam Arts Council (cat.), and *Young Blood*, Riverside Studios, London, 1983; *Metaphor and/or Symbol*, National Museum of Modern Art, Tokyo, and National Museum of Modern Art, Osaka (cat.), and *Home and Abroad*, Serpentine Gallery, London, 1984; *The Irresistible Object*, Leeds City Art Gallery, England, and *Space Invaders*, The Makenzie Art Gallery, Regina, Canada (cat.), 1985; *Time after Time*, Diane Brown Gallery, New York, *Sculpture: Nine Artists from Britain*, Louisiana Museum, Copenhagen, and *Drawings by Sculptors*, Nohra Haime Gallery, New York, 1986. Currently lives and works in London.

Selected publications include Raymond Tio Belido, "New English Sculpture," *Axe Sud*, Winter 1982; Stuart Morgan, "Edward Allington," *Artforum*, November 1983; Finella Crichton, "Interview with Edward Allington," *Artscribe*, July/August 1985; Caroline Collier, "Times Chariots," *Studio International*, 1985.

Siah Armajani

Born in Teheran, Iran, in 1939. Selected one-person exhibitions include *Siah Armajani: Architectural Entities*, Gallery of Visual Arts, University of Montana, Missoula, 1970; *Siah Armajani: Red School House for Thomas Paine*, Philadelphia College of Art, 1978 (cat.); New Gallery of Contemporary Art, Cleveland, and Ohio State University, Columbus, 1979; Max Protetch Gallery, New York, 1981, 1983, 1984; *Siah Armajani: Bridges, Houses, Communal Spaces, Dictionary for Building*, Institute of Contemporary Art, University of Pennsylvania, Philadelphia, 1985 (cat.). Selected group exhibitions include *Art by Telephone*, Museum of Contemporary Art, Chicago, and *Painting and Sculpture Today, 1969*, Indianapolis Museum of Art, 1969 (cat.); *Art in the Mind*, Allen Art Museum, Oberlin College, Ohio (cat.), and *Information*, The Museum of Modern Art, New York, 1970 (cat.); *The Boardwalk Show*, Convention Hall, Atlantic City, New Jersey, and *Works for New Spaces*, Walker Art Center, Minneapolis, 1971 (cat.); *Sculpture for a New Era*, Federal Center, Chicago, 1975 (cat.); *Virtual Reality*, Carpenter Center for Visual Arts, Harvard University, Cambridge, Massachusetts, 1976; *Scale and Environment: 10 Sculptors*, Walker Art Center, Minneapolis, 1977 (cat.); *Architectural Analogues*, Whitney Museum of American Art, Downtown Branch, New York (cat.), and *Dwellings*, Institute of Contemporary Art, University of Pennsylvania, Philadelphia, 1978 (cat.); *Architectural Sculpture*, Los Angeles Institute of Contemporary Art, 1980; *Metaphor: New Projects by Contemporary Sculptors*, Hirshhorn Museum and Sculpture Garden, Smithsonian Institution, Washington, D.C., 1981 (cat.); *Documenta 7*, Kassel, Federal Republic of Germany, 1982; *New Art*, The Tate Gallery, London, 1983 (cat.); *An International Survey of*

Recent Painting and Sculpture, The Museum of Modern Art, New York (cat.), and *Content: A Contemporary Focus 1974–1984*, Hirshhorn Museum and Sculpture Garden, Smithsonian Institution, Washington, D.C., 1984 (cat.); *The Artists as Social Designer: Aspects of Public Urban Art Today*, Los Angeles County Museum of Art, 1985. Currently lives and works in Minneapolis, Minnesota.

Selected publications include Joachim Neugroschel, "Siah Armajani," *Arts Magazine*, March 1970; Robert Pincus-Witten, "Siah Armajani: Populist Mechanics," *Arts Magazine*, October 1978; John Ashbery, "Armajani: East Meets West," *Newsweek*, April 4, 1983; Calvin Thompkins, "The Art World: Perception at All Levels," *The New Yorker*, December 3, 1984.

Roger Brown

Born in 1941 in Hamilton, Alabama. Selected one-person exhibitions include Phyllis Kind Gallery, Chicago, 1971, 1973, 1974, 1976–77, 1979, 1982, 1984; Peale House, Pennsylvania Academy of Fine Arts, Philadelphia, and Galerie Dathea Speyer, Paris, 1974; Phyllis Kind Gallery, New York, 1975, 1979, 1981, 1982, 1984; *Currents 6: Roger Brown*, The Saint Louis Art Museum (cat.), *Roger Brown: Matrix/Berkeley 35*, University Art Museum, University of California, Berkeley (cat.), and *Roger Brown*, Montgomery Museum of Fine Arts, Alabama, 1980 (cat.); Asher/Faure Gallery, Los Angeles, 1983; *Roger Brown: Selected Paintings 1973–1983*, Nexus Contemporary Art Center, Atlanta, 1984 (cat.). Selected group exhibitions include *The Spirit of the Comics*, Institute of Contemporary Art, University of Pennsylvania, Philadelphia, 1969 (cat.); *Painting and Sculpture Today 1972*, Indianapolis Museum of Art, 1972 (cat.); *Extraordinary Realities*, Whitney Museum of American Art, New York (cat.), and *Made in Chicago*, XII Bienal de Sao Paolo, Brazil, 1973 (cat.); *1974 Biennial Exhibition*, Whitney Museum of American Art, New York, 1974 (cat.); *View of a Decade*, Museum of Contemporary Art, Chicago, 1977 (cat.); *American Painting of the 1970s*, Albright-Knox Art Gallery, Buffalo, 1978 (cat.); *Intricate Structure/Repeated Image*, Tyler School of Art, Temple University, Philadelphia, 1979 (cat.); *The Figurative Tradition and the Whitney Museum of American Art: Painting and Sculpture from the Permanent Collection*, Whitney Museum of American Art, New York, 1980 (cat.); *From Chicago*, Pace Gallery, New York, 1982 (cat.); *Notable Acquisitions 1982–83*, Metropolitan Museum of Art, New York, 1983 (cat.); *An International Survey of Recent Painting and Sculpture*, The Museum of Modern Art, New York (cat.), and *Content: A Contemporary Focus 1974–1984*, Hirshhorn Museum and Sculpture Garden, Smithsonian Institution, Washington, D.C., 1984 (cat.); *The 39th*

Biennial Exhibition of Contemporary American Painting, The Corcoran Gallery of Art, Washington, D.C., 1985 (cat.). Currently lives and works in Chicago.

Selected publications include Henry Gerrit, "New York Reviews: Roger Brown," *Artnews*, December 1977; Barry Blinderman, "A Conversation with Roger Brown," *Arts Magazine*, May 1981; Harry Hanson, "The World According to Roger Brown," *Portfolio*, September–October 1981; Carter Ratcliff, "Roger Brown at Phyllis Kind," *Art in America*, May 1984.

Harry Fritzius

Born in 1932 in Blytheville, Arkansas. Selected one-person exhibitions include Richard L. Nelson Gallery, University of California, Davis, 1985; Bruce Velick Gallery, San Francisco, 1985; Bruce Velick Gallery, New York, 1986; *Centric 22: Harry Fritzius*, University Art Museum, California State University, Long Beach, 1986; Bruce Velick Gallery, San Francisco, 1986. Selected group exhibitions include *Public and Private: American Prints Today*, Brooklyn Museum, New York, 1986; *Third Western States Biennial*, organized by the Western States Foundation and traveling nationally. Currently lives and works in San Francisco.

Selected publications include Kenneth Baker, "Fritzius Remakes Old Art in New Forms," *San Francisco Chronicle*, September 30, 1985; Bill Berkson, "Harry Fritzius," *Artforum*, December 1985; David S. Rubin, "Fritzius at Bruce Velick," *Art in America*, January 1986.

Douglas Higgins

Born in 1952 in Roanoke, Virginia. Selected one-person exhibitions include Roanoke Fine Arts Center, Virginia, 1975 and 1976; duPont Gallery, Washington and Lee University, Lexington, Virginia, 1977 and 1979; Marsh Gallery, University of Richmond, Virginia, 1979 and 1980; Sweet Briar College, Virginia, 1982; *Douglas Higgins: Works from Rome 1981–1982*, Siegel Contemporary Art, New York, 1982; *Masters of Drawing II: Douglas Higgins*, Anderson Gallery, Virginia Commonwealth University, Richmond, 1983; *Douglas Higgins: Eros Kalos—Works from 1983–1984*, Siegel Contemporary Art, New York, 1984. Selected group exhibitions include *'40–'80: Forty Years of Funding to Artists in Virginia*, Virginia Museum of Fine Arts, Richmond, 1980 (cat.); *The Next Juried Show: Painting and Sculpture*, Virginia Museum of Fine Arts, Richmond, 1983 (cat.); *Salvo*, Ruth Siegel, Ltd., New York, and *Masters of Contemporary Drawing*, Salisbury State College, Maryland, 1984 (cat.); *Surplus: Today's Art in an Overpopulated City*, Exit Art, New York, 1985, and *Four Painters from New York*,

Janet Steinberg Gallery, San Francisco, and *The Classic Tradition in Recent Painting and Sculpture*, The Aldrich Museum of Contemporary Art, Ridgefield, Connecticut, 1985 (cat.); *Olympus Revisited*, Summit Art Center, New Jersey, 1986 (cat.). Currently lives and works in Andover, Massachusetts, and Richmond, Virginia.

Selected publications include Gerald D. Silk, "Douglas Higgins," *Arts Magazine*, January 1983; Ellen Lee Klein, "Arts Reviews: Douglas Higgins," *Arts Magazine*, September 1984; Kenneth Baker, "New Paintings in Search of a Purpose," *San Francisco Chronicle*, May 29, 1985.

David Hollowell

Born in 1951 in Hornell, New York. Selected one-person exhibitions include Paul Mellon Center, Wallingford, Connecticut, 1976; Fontbonne College Gallery, St. Louis, 1978; Schweig Gallery, St. Louis, 1980; Rosewall Museum and Art Center, Minnesota, 1982; Jane Haslem Gallery, Washington, D.C., and Schaefer Gallery, Gustavus Adolphus College, St. Peter, Minnesota, 1983; *David Hollowell: Paintings, Drawings, Pastels*, Jane Haslem Gallery, Washington, D.C. (cat.), and Brunswick Gallery, Missoula, Montana, 1985. Selected group exhibitions include Steinberg Gallery, Washington University, St. Louis, 1976; Marilyn Pearl Gallery, New York, 1977; University of North Carolina, Greenville, 1979; Messing Gallery, St. Louis, 1980; Little Rock Art Museum, Arkansas, 1981; *American Painters: Figuration*, Jane Haslem Gallery, Washington, D.C., 1985 (cat.); Gallery Paule Anglim, San Francisco, 1986. Currently lives and works in Davis, California.

Selected publications include Jane Addams Allen, "A Touch of The Dutch in Hollowell Paintings," *Washington Times,* April 1983; Jo Ann Lewis, "Classic Poses of Hollowell," *Washington Post,* January 4, 1986.

Komar and Melamid

Vitaly Komar was born in 1943 in Moscow. Aleksandr Melamid was born in 1945 in Moscow. Selected solo exhibitions include Moscow Institute for Art and Design, 1967; Ronald Feldman Fine Arts, Inc., New York, 1976-80, 1984, 1985; Ohio University Gallery of Fine Arts, Columbus, 1977; White Gallery, Tel Aviv, Israel, and Israel Museum, Jerusalem, 1978; Edwin A. Ulrich Museum of Art, Wichita State University, Kansas; *Komar and Melamid*, Portland Center for Visual Arts, Oregon, 1983; *Komar and Melamid: Stalin and the Muses*, Saidye Bronfman Center, Montreal, and *Komar and Melamid's Version of Russian History*, University of Iowa Museum of Art, Iowa City, 1984; *Komar and Melamid*, Metropolitan Museum

and Art Center, Coral Gables, Florida, and *Komar and Melamid*, The Fruitmarket Gallery, Edinburgh, Scotland, 1985; *Komar and Melamid*, Arts Council Gallery, Belfast, Ireland, 1986. Selected group exhibitions include *The Museum of Drawers*, Israel Museum, Jerusalem, 1977; *New Art from the Soviet Union*, Pratt Manhattan Center Gallery, New York, and *Artist and Society*, Tel Aviv Museum, Israel, 1978; *Messages: Words and Images*, Freedman Gallery, Albright College, Reading, Pennsylvania, 1981; *Face to Face*, Alternative Museum, New York, and *Counterparts and Affinities*, Metropolitan Museum of of Art, New York, 1982; *New Acquisitions*, The Museum of Modern Art, New York, 1983; *Artistic Collaboration in the Twentieth Century*, Hirshhorn Museum and Sculpture Garden, Smithsonian Institution, Washington, D.C. (cat.), and *An International Survey of Recent Painting and Sculpture*, The Museum of Modern Art, New York (cat.), and *Content: A Contemporary Focus 1974–84*, Hirshhorn Museum and Sculpture Garden, Smithsonian Institution, Washington, D.C., 1984 (cat.); *Synaesthetics: Collaborations between Artists and Writers*, P.S. 1, The Institute for Art and Urban Resources, New York, and *The Classic Spirit 1985*, Martina Hamilton Gallery, New York, 1985; Ronald Feldman Fine Arts, Inc., New York, and *Sots Art*, The New Museum of Contemporary Art, New York, 1986 (cat.). Both artists currently live and work in New York.

Selected publications include Hedrick Smith, "Young Soviet Painters Score Socialist Art," *The New York Times*, March 19, 1974; Jamey Gambrell, "Komar and Melamid: From Behind the Ironical Curtain," *Artforum*, April 1982; Douglas Davis, "Nuclear Visions," *Vogue*, November 1984; Peter Schjedahl, "Komar/Melamid," *Flash Art*, December 1985.

Christopher Le Brun

Born in 1951 in Portsmouth, England. Selected one-person exhibitions include *Christopher Le Brun: Drawings*, Nigel Greenwood Gallery, London, 1980; Gillespie-Laage-Salomon, Paris, 1981; Nigel Greenwood Gallery, London, 1982; Sperone Westwater Gallery, New York, 1983 (cat.); Nigel Greenwood Gallery, London, The Fruitmarket Gallery, Edinburgh, and *Christopher Le Brun: Paintings*, Arnolfini Gallery, Bristol, England, 1985 (cat.); Kunsthalle, Basel, 1986. Selected group exhibitions include *London Group*, Camden Arts Centre, Camden, England, 1975; *John Moores Liverpool Exhibition XI*, Walker Art Gallery, Liverpool, 1978; *Summer Show III*, Serpentine Gallery, London, 1979; Nigel Greenwood Gallery, London, and *Nuova Immagine*, Palazzo della Triennale, Milan, 1980; *Enciclodpedia*, Galleria Civica, Modena, Italy, and *Fragments against Ruins*, Arts Council of Great Britain, London, 1981; *Sydney*

Biennale, Australia, and *Aperto 82*, Venice Biennale, Italy, 1982; *The Granada Collection: Recent British Paintings and Drawings*, Whitworth Art Gallery, Manchester, England, and *New Art*, Tate Gallery, London, 1983; *Arte allo Specchio*, Venice Biennale, Italy, and *An International Survey of Recent Painting and Sculpture*, The Museum of Modern Art, New York, 1984 (cat.); *Romanticism and Primitivism in Art*, Jan Eric Lowendaller Gallery, New York, and *Modern Landscape*, Sunderland Arts Centre, England, 1985. Currently lives and works in London.

Selected publications include Adrian Searle, "Christopher Le Brun at Nigel Greenwood Gallery," *Artscribe*, June 1982; Donald Kuspit, "Christopher Le Brun," *Artforum*, December 1983; Michael Kohn, "Christopher Le Brun," *Flash Art*, January 1984; Caroline Collier, " White Horses … Christopher Le Brun," *Studio International*, vol. 198, no. 1010, 1985.

Carlo Maria Mariani

Born in 1931 in Rome. Selected one-person exhibitions include *Iper/ri/cognizione*, Galleria d'arte Seconda Scala, Rome, 1973; *Compendio di pittura*, Cannaviello Studio d'arte, Rome, 1975; *Affinità elettive*, Ghiringhelli/Sperone, Rome, and *Pictor philosophus*, Paul Maenz, Cologne, 1977; *Artiges Kind*, Paolo Sproviere, Rome, 1979; *Costellazione del Leone*, Gian Enzo Sperone, Rome, and Sperone Westwater Fisher, New York, 1981; Mario Diacono, Rome, and Artra/Studio, Milan, 1983; Sperone Westwater, New York, 1984; Natalie Seroussi, Paris, 1985. Selected group exhibitions include *Mostra d'arte Sacra*, Cenobio Visualita, Milan, 1973; *Grafica iperrealista internazionale*, Cannaviello Studio d'arte, Rome, 1974; *Foto & Idea*, Commune di Pama, Galleria Comunale d'Arte Moderna and Sala del Ridotto del Teatro Regina, Parma, Italy, 1976; *Arte/Storia dell'Arte*, Galleria Peccolo, Livorno, Italy; *Arte e Critica 1980*, Galleria Nazionale d'Arte Moderna, Rome, 1980; *Drawings*, Sperone Westwater Fisher, New York, 1981; *Documenta 7*, Kassel, Federal Republic of Germany, 1982; *Via New York*, Musee d'Art Contemporain, Montreal, and *Content: A Contemporary Focus 1974–1984*, Hirshhorn Museum and Sculpture Garden, Smithsonian Institution, Washington, D.C., 1984 (cat.); National Museum of Modern Art, Tokyo, 1985. Currently lives and works in Rome.

Selected publications include Michael Kohn, "Carlo Maria Mariani and Neoclassicism," *Arts Magazine*, January 1982; Danny Berger, "Carlo Maria Mariani in His Studio in Rome: An Interview," *Print Collector's Newsletter*, July-August 1984; Henry Martin, "Inside Europe: Italy," *Artnews*, February 1985.

Ann McCoy

Born in 1946 in Boulder, Colorado. Selected one-person exhibitions include *Ann McCoy: Recent Work*, Fourcade-Droll, New York, 1974; *Ann McCoy: Large Drawings and Lithographs*, Institute of Contemporary Art, Boston, 1975; *Underwater Drawings*, Margo Leavin Gallery, Los Angeles, 1976; Chandler Coventry Gallery, Paddington, Australia, 1978; *Ann McCoy: Night Sea Series*, Brooke Alexander, Inc., New York, and *The Red Sea & The Night Sea*, Arts Club of Chicago, 1979; *Ann McCoy: The Underworld*, Brooke Alexander, Inc., New York, 1981; *Ann McCoy*, Metropolitan Museum of Art, New York, 1982; *Ann McCoy*, Art Gallery, Fine Arts Center, State University of New York at Stony Brook, 1983; Brooke Alexander, Inc., New York, 1985. Selected group exhibitions include *15 Young Artists*, Pasadena Art Museum, California, 1972; *Six Visions*, Institute of Contemporary Art, University of Pennsylvania, Philadelphia, and *New American Landscapes*, Vassar College Art Gallery, Poughkeepsie, New York, 1973; *Painting and Sculpture Today 1974*, Indianapolis Museum of Art, and *Drawings: An Exhibition of Works by Contemporary Artists*, Nancy Hoffman Gallery, New York, 1974; *America 1976*, Corcoran Gallery of Art, Washington, D.C., 1976; *Decade in Review*, Whitney Museum of American Art, New York, 1979; *On Paper*, Virginia Museum of Fine Arts, Richmond, 1980; *New New York*, University Fine Arts Galleries, Florida State University, Tallahassee, 1982; *Shift: LA/NY*, Newport Harbor Art Museum, Newport Beach, California, 1983; *Memento Mori*, Moore College of Art Gallery, Philadelphia, 1985. Currently lives and works in New York.

Selected publications include Melinda Terbell, "The Strangeness of Reality," *Artnews*, November 1973; Jean Luc-Dordeaux, "The Silent World of Ann McCoy," *Art International*, January 1977; Hilton Kramer, "Ann McCoy," *The New York Times*, October 12, 1980; Melinda Wortz, "The LA/NY Shift: For Some Artists, the Fast Lane Heads East," *Artnews*, January 1983.

Stephen McKenna

Born in 1939 in London. Selected one-person exhibitions include Galerie Olaf Hudtwalcker, Frankfurt, 1964; Galerie Ostentor, Dortmund, Federal Republic of Germany, 1971; Galerie Rutzmoser, Munich, 1974; Sander Gallery, Washington, D.C., and Barry Barker Gallery, London, 1978; Association for the Museum of Contemporary Art, Ghent, Belgium, 1980; The Arts Council of Northern Ireland, Belfast, 1981; Sander Gallery, New York, 1983; Galerie Springer, Berlin, and *Stephen McKenna Retrospective 1979–1984*, Stedelijk van Abbesmuseum, Eindhoven, the Netherlands, 1984; Institute of Contemporary Arts, London, and Sander Gallery, New York, 1985 (cat.). Selected group exhibitions include *Towards Another Picture*, Midland Group Gallery, Nottingham, England, 1977; *Europa '79*, Kunst der 80er Jahre, Stuttgart, Federal Republic of Germany, 1979; *British Art 1940–1980*, Hayward Gallery, London, 1980; *Documenta 7*, Kassel, Federal Republic of Germany, 1982; *New Art*, Tate Gallery, London, 1983; *The British Art Show*, Birmingham, England, 1984; *The Classic Tradition in Recent Painting and Sculpture*, The Aldrich Museum of Contemporary Art, Ridgefield, Connecticut, 1985 (cat.). Currently lives and works in London and Brussels.

Selected publications include Angela Vettese, "Europe and America: Two Aspects of the New Surreal," *Flash Art*, April/May 1985; Bernhard Schulz, "Stephen McKenna," *Flash Art*, Summer 1985; Lisa Liebmann, "Misty Channels," *Artforum*, October 1985; Maurice Poirier, "Stephen McKenna," *Artnews*, February 1986.

Odd Nerdrum

Born in 1945 in Norway. Selected one-person exhibitions include Stavanger Faste Gallery, Norway, 1969; Gallerie 27, Norway, 1971; Kunstnerforbundet, Oslo, 1973, 1976, 1980; The Bedford Way Gallery, London, 1982; Gallery Tanum, Norway, 1983; Delaware Art Museum, Wilmington, 1985; Germans Van Eck Gallery, New York, and Martina Hamilton Gallery, 1986. Selected group exhibitions include Kurturhuset, Stockholm, 1979; *The Classic Tradition in Recent Painting and Sculpture*, The Aldrich Museum of Contemporary Art, Ridgefield, Connecticut, 1985 (cat.); *Neo-Neoclassicism*, Edith C. Blum Art Institute, Bard College, Annandale, New York, 1986.

Selected publications include Donald Kuspit, "The Aging of the Immediate," *Arts Magazine*, September 1984; Maurice Poirier, "Odd Nerdrum," *Artnews*, September 1985; Eleanor Heartney, "Apocalyptic Visions, Arcadian Dreams," *Artnews*, January 1986; John Russell, "Odd Nerdrum," *The New York Times*, May 16, 1986.

Giulio Paolini

Born in 1940 in Genoa, Italy. Selected one-person exhibitions include Galleria La Salita, Rome, 1964; Galleria dell'Ariete, Milan, 1966; Studio La Tartaruga, Rome, 1969; Galleria Notizie, Turin, Italy, 1970 (cat.); Royal College of Art, London, and Studio Marconi, Milan, 1973 (cat.); The Museum of Modern Art, New York, 1974 (cat.); Galerie Art in Progress, Monaco, and Galerie Paul Maenz, Cologne, Federal Republic of Germany, 1975; Sperone Westwater Fischer Gallery, New York, 1977; Lisson Gallery, London, 1979; Stedelijk Abbemuseum, Amsterdam, and Museum of Modern Art, Oxford, England, 1980 (cat.); Raum für Kunst, Hamburg, Federal Republic of Germany, 1982 (cat.); Los Angeles Institute of Contemporary Art, 1984; Pinacoteca Comunale, Ravenna, Italy (cat.), and Marian Goodman Gallery, New York, 1985. Selected group exhibitions include *International Exhibition of Drawings*, Mayaguez, Puerto Rico, 1968; *Information*, The Museum of Modern Art, New York, 1970; *Arte povera*, Kunstverein, Munich, and *New Italian Art: 1953–71*, Walker Art Gallery, Liverpool, England, 1971; *XII Bienal*, Sao Paulo, Brazil, and *An Exhibition of New Italian Art*, The Arts Council of Northern Ireland Gallery, Belfast, 1973; *La cosa disegnata*, Studio Marconi, Milan, 1976; *Documenta 6*, Kassel, Federal Republic of Germany, and *Rose '77: The Poetry of Vision*, Hugh Lane Municipal Gallery of Modern Art, Dublin, 1977; *Genealogia*, Studio Marconi, Milan, 1980; *Murs*, Centre Georges Pompidou, Paris, and *Baselitz, Kounellis, Paolini, Penck*, Galleria Christian Stein, Turin, Italy, 1981; *'60–'80*, Stedelijk Museum, Amsterdam, and *A Selection of the Acquisitions*, The Tate Gallery, London, and *Documenta 7*, Kassel, Federal Republic of Germany, 1982; *The Knot: Arte Povera at P.S. 1*, P.S. 1, The Institute for Art and Urban Resources, New York, 1985 (cat.). Currently lives and works in Turin, Italy.

Selected publications include M. Bandini, "Interview with Giulio Paolini," *Prospects* (Milan), 1972; M. Volpi Orlandini, "Giulio Paolini," *Futuribili* (Rome), 1972; F. Caroli, "Parola-Immagine," *Fabri* (Milan), 1979; B. Marcelis, "Interview with Giulio Paolini," *Domus* (Milan), 1980.

Earl Staley

Born in 1938 in Oak Park, Illinois. Selected one-person exhibitions include Illinois Wesleyan University, Bloomington, 1960; Downstairs Gallery, St. Louis, 1966; Rice University, Houston, 1967; David Gallery, Houston, 1972; Sarah Campbell Blaffer Gallery, University of Houston, and Texas Gallery, Houston, 1974, 1975, 1977, 1978; *Earl Staley: Mythologies*, Perspectives Gallery, Contemporary Art Museum, Houston, 1980; Phyllis Kind Gallery, New York, 1981; *Earl Staley: 1973–1983*, Contemporary Art Museum, Houston, 1983; *Earl Staley: Arrivederci Roma*, Watson/de Nagy & Company, Houston, 1985. Selected group exhibitions include *29th American Graphics Show*, University of Kansas, Lawrence; *National Exhibition of Contemporary Art*, The Oklahoma Museum of Art, Oklahoma City, 1962; *Kansas City Art Institute Invitational*, Missouri, 1966; *Abstract Painting and Sculpture in Houston*, The Museum of Fine Arts, Houston, 1974; *1975 Biennial Exhibition: Contemporary American Art*, Whitney Museum of American

Art, New York, 1975 (cat.); *The Philadelphia-Houston Exchange*, Institute of Contemporary Art, University of Pennsylvania, Philadelphia, 1976 (cat.); *1980 Houston Area Exhibition*, Sarah Campbell Blaffer Gallery, University of Houston, 1980; *New Figuration in America*, Milwaukee Art Museum, 1982 (cat.); *Paradise Lost/Paradise Regained: American Visions of the New Decade*, American Pavilion, Venice Biennale, Italy, and *Content: A Contemporary Focus 1974–84*, Hirshhorn Museum and Sculpture Garden, Smithsonian Institution, Washington, D.C., 1984 (cat.); *Fresh Paint: The Houston School*, The Museum of Fine Arts, Houston, 1985 (cat.). Currently lives and works in Houston.

Selected publications include Jozanne Raybor, "Review of Exhibitions—Houston: Earl Staley," *Art in America*, September–October 1974; Susan Platt, "Earl Staley, New Work," *Artweek*, March 22, 1980; Carol J. Everingham, "Earl Staley's Paintings Multiflavored," *The Houston Post*, December 11, 1983; Suzanne Bloom, "Review: Earl Staley at Watson de Nagy & Co.," *Artforum*, Summer 1985.

M. Louise Stanley

Born in 1942 in Charleston, West Virginia. Selected one-person exhibitions include University of California, Berkeley, 1971; Matrix Project, University Art Museum, University of California, Berkeley, and P.S. 1, The Institute for Art and Urban Resources, New York, 1978; Interart Gallery, Women's Interart Center, Inc., New York, 1980; James Crumley Gallery, Mira Costa College, Oceanside, California, and Quay Gallery, San Francisco, 1982, 1983; Bransten Gallery, San Francisco, 1986. Selected group exhibitions include *A Show of Hands*, California College of Arts and Crafts, Oakland, 1970; *Paintings on Paper*, San Francisco Art Institute, 1971; *Market Street Project*, Newport Harbor Art Museum, Newport Beach, California, 1973; *Narrative Art*, Lone Mountain College, San Francisco, 1976; *Touching All Things*, Civic Arts Gallery, Walnut Creek, California, 1977; *The Work Show*, Downtown Center, Fine Arts Museums of San Francisco, 1978; *Humor*, Palo Alto Cultural Center, California, and *Bay Area Painting Invitational*, Richmond Art Center, California, 1979; *Drawings by Painters*, Long Beach Museum of Art, California, 1982; *The Impolite Figure*, Southern Exposure Gallery, San Francisco, 1983; *Modern Romances*, Reese Bullen Gallery, Humboldt State University, California, and *Seven Narrative Painters*, Mills College Art Gallery, Oakland, 1984. Currently lives and works in Oakland.

Selected publications include Judith Dunham, "Foibles and Fabrications," *Artweek*, March 29, 1980; Suzaan Boettger, "The Impolite Figure," *Artforum*, October 1983; David Winter, "Artists the Critics are Watching," *Artnews*, November 1984; David S. Rubin, "M. Louise Stanley at Rena Bransten Gallery," *Art in America*, April 1986.

Pat Steir

Born in 1940 in Newark, New Jersey. One-person exhibitions include Terry Dintenfass Gallery, New York, 1964; Douglass College Art Gallery, Rutgers University, New Brunswick, New Jersey, 1972; Fourcade, Droll, Inc., New York, and John Doyle Gallery, Paris, 1975; Galerie Farideh Cadot, Paris, and Galerie Marilena Bonomo, Bari, Italy, 1978; Max Protetch Gallery, New York, 1980, 1981, 1983; *Pat Steir: Recent Paintings*, Bell Gallery, List Art Center, Brown University, Providence, Rhode Island, 1981 (cat.); *Form, Illusion, Myth: The Prints and Drawings of Pat Steir*, Spencer Museum of Art, University of Kansas, Lawrence (cat.), and *Arbitrary Order: Paintings by Pat Steir*, Contemporary Art Museum, Houston, 1983 (cat.); *The Breughel Series (A Vanitas of Style)*, Brooklyn Museum, New York, 1984; Minneapolis College of Art and Design, Minnesota, 1985; Fuller Goldeen Gallery, San Francisco, 1985, 1986; Castelli Graphics, New York, 1986. Selected group exhibitions include the High Museum of Art, 1963; *Three Paintings*, Paley & Lowe, Inc., New York, 1971; *Painting and Sculpture Today, 1972*, Indianapolis Museum of Art, Indiana, 1972 (cat.); *Biennial Exhibition: Contemporary American Art*, Whitney Museum of American Art, New York, 1973 (cat.); *Joan Snyder and Pat Steir*, Institute of Contemporary Art, Boston, and *Inaugural Exhibition*, Loretta Yarlow Fine Arts, Ltd., Toronto, 1974; *16 Projects/4 Artists*, The University Art Museum, California State University, Long Beach, 1976; *America Drawn and Matched*, The Museum of Modern Art, New York, 1977; *Artist and Printer: Six American Print Studios*, Walker Art Center, Minneapolis, 1980 (cat.); *Post Minimalisms*, The Aldrich Museum of Contemporary Art, Ridgefield, Connecticut, 1982; *1983 Biennial Exhibition*, Whitney Museum of American Art, New York, 1983 (cat.); *Content: A Contemporary Focus 1974–1984*, Hirshhorn Museum and Sculpture Garden, Smithsonian Institution, Washington, D.C., 1984 (cat.); *New Work on Paper 3*, The Museum of Modern Art, New York, 1985; *The New Culture: Woman Artists of the Seventies*, University of Akron, Ohio, 1986. Currently lives and works in New York and Amsterdam.

Selected publications include Marcia Tucker, "An Interview with Pat Steir," *Journal of the Los Angeles Institute of Contemporary Art*, March–April 1976; John Perricault, "Report from Micronesia: Panoply of Ponape," *Art in America*, May 1980; Joan Simon, "Expressionism Today: An Artist's Symposium," *Art in America*, December 1982; Christine Temlin, "Steir Shows Continuity," *The Boston Globe*, May 22, 1986.

Michelle Stuart

Born in Los Angeles. Selected one-person exhibitions include Douglass College, Rutgers University, New Brunswick, New Jersey, 1973; Max Hutchinson Gallery, New York, 1974, 1975, 1976; Massachusetts Institute of Technology, Cambridge, 1977; Institute of Contemporary Art, Nash House, London, 1979 (cat.); Galerie Aronowitch, Stockholm, 1980; Susan Caldwell Gallery, New York, 1982; Haags Gemeentemuseum, The Hague, the Netherlands, and *Michelle Stuart: Place and Time*, Walker Art Center, Minneapolis, 1983 (cat.); Galerie Krista Mikkola, Helsinki, 1984; Art Club of Chicago, 1986 (cat.). Selected group exhibitions include *Outsize Drawings*, Loeb Art Center, New York University, New York, 1972; *Painting and Sculpture Today, 1974*, Indianapolis Museum of Art, Indiana, 1974 (cat.); *Report from Soho*, Grey Art Gallery, New York University, New York, 1975; *Handmade Paper*, The Museum of Modern Art, New York, 1976; *Artist's Books*, Mandeville Art Gallery, University of California, San Diego, 1977; *The Great Big Drawings Show*, P.S. 1, The Institute for Art and Urban Resources, New York, 1979; *With Paper about Paper*, Albright-Knox Art Gallery, Buffalo, New York, 1980 (cat.); *New American Paperwork*, National Museum of Modern Art, Kyoto, 1983; *Primitivism in 20th Century Art: Affinities of the Tribal and the Modern*, The Museum of Modern Art, New York, 1984 (cat.); *Contemporary American Prints: Recent Acquisitions*, The Brooklyn Museum, New York, 1985. Currently lives and works in New York.

Selected publications include Lawrence Alloway, "Michelle Stuart: A Fabric of Significations," *Artforum*, January 1974; Jacquiline Brody, "Artist's Books: Michelle Stuart, The Fall," *Print Collectors' Newsletter*, March–April 1977; Ellen Lubell, "Michelle Stuart: Icons from the Archives of Times," *Arts Magazine*, June 1979. Glen Reed, "Michelle Stuart Patches Together an Art of Nature," *Sunday Camera*, July 21, 1985.

Mark Tansey

Born in 1949 in San Jose, California. Selected one-person exhibitions include Grace Borgenicht Gallery, New York, 1982, 1984; John Berggruen Gallery, San Francisco, and Contemporary Arts Museum, Houston, 1984. Selected group exhibitions include *Artists of P.S. 122*, Fifth Street Gallery, New York, 1978; *Selections 12*, The Drawing Center, New York, 1980; *Nut Just for Laughs*, The New Museum of Contemporary Art, New York, 1981; *Painting and Sculpture Today 1982*, Indianapolis Museum of Art, Indiana, 1982 (cat.); *1983 Biennial Exhibition*, Whitney Museum of American Art, New York (cat.), and *Recent Acquisitions*, The Museum of Modern Art, New York, 1983; *An International Survey of Recent Painting and Sculpture*, The Museum of Modern Art, New York, 1984 (cat.); *The Car Show*, Museum of Contemporary Art, Los Angeles (cat.), and *Figure in Contemporary American Art*, Metropolitan Museum of Art, New York, 1985; *Inaugural Exhibition*, Curt Marcus Gallery, New York, 1986. Currently lives and works in New York.

Selected publications include Kay Larson, "Ways with Wit," *New York Magazine*, November 15, 1982; Richard Armstrong, "Reviews: Mark Tansey," *Artforum*, February 1983; Kate Linker, "Multiple Choice," *Artforum*, September 1983; John Russell, "Mark Tansey," *The New York Times*, March 9, 1984.

Collector's Forum

Collectors Forum Biennial Committee, 1986

Gardiner Hempel
Cochairman

Chotsie Blank
Cochairman

Jim Ludwig
Fund Raising Cochairman

Hendy Henderson
Fund Raising Cochairman

Helen Schwab
Fund Raising

Howard Leach
Fund Raising

Bobbie Wilsey
Fund Raising

Eileen Ludwig
Pre-Opening Celebration Chairman

Robin Quist
Pre-Opening Celebration

Gretchen Leach
Pre-Opening Celebration

Pat Falvey
Pre-Opening Celebration

Cynthia Coolidge
Pre-Opening Celebration

Elaine McKeon
Symposium Chairman

Barrie Ramsay
Symposium

Eileen McKeon
Symposium

Byron R. Meyer
Public Relations Chairman

Frances Bowes
Public Relations

Jerry Kingsley
Public Relations

Museum Biennial Committee, 1986

Graham W. J. Beal
Chief Curator

Henry T. Hopkins
Consultant

Kathleen Rydar
Fund Raising

Robert Whyte
Symposium

Marcia Tanner
Public Relations

Jo Rowlings
Public Relations

Michael Schwager
Curatorial Assistant

Oni Berglund
Coordinator

Collectors Forum

Mr. and Mrs. Joachim Bechtle

Mr. Gerson Bakar

Mr. and Mrs. Allan Blank

Mr. and Mrs. Roger Boas

Mr. and Mrs. John G. Bowes

Mr. and Mrs. Brook Byers

Mr. and Mrs. Carlton Coolidge

Mr. and Mrs. John Crichton

Mr. and Mrs. Thomas Davis

Mr. and Mrs. Rene di Rosa

Mr. and Mrs. William Edwards

Mr. and Mrs. Jack Falvey

Mr. and Mrs. Donald G. Fisher

Mr. and Mrs. Robert Fisher

Mr. and Mrs. Richard Goldman

Dr. and Mrs. Richard Gonzalez

Dr. Margot Hedden Green

Dr. and Mrs. Robert L. Green

Mr. and Mrs. Peter Haas

Mr. and Mrs. Walter A. Haas, Jr.

Mr. Frank O. Hamilton

Mr. Gardiner Hempel

Mr. Wellington S. Henderson, Jr.

Mrs. Barbara P. Hilliard

Mr. and Mrs. Franklin Johnson

Mr. and Mrs. Jerrold Kingsley

Mr. and Mrs. Richard Kramlich

Mr. and Mrs. Howard Leach

Mrs. Philip E. Lilienthal

Mr. and Mrs. James J. Ludwig

Mr. and Mrs. John McGuire

Ms. Eileen McKeon

Mrs. Elaine McKeon

Mr. Byron Meyer

Mr. and Mrs. Themis Michos

Mr. and Mrs. Stuart G. Moldaw

Ms. Diane Morris

Mr. and Mrs. Mervin Morris

Mr. and Mrs. Gibson Myers

Mr. and Mrs. Blair Pascoe

Mrs. George Quist

Mrs. Barrie Ramsay

Mrs. Ellen Davies Rush

Mrs. Madeline Haas Russell

Mrs. Norma Schlesinger

Mr. and Mrs. Albert R. Schreck

Mr. and Mrs. Charles Schwab

Mr. and Mrs. Donald Scutchfield

Mr. and Mrs. Jan Shrem

Mr. and Mrs. Kenneth Siebel

Mr. and Mrs. Philip Smith

Mr. and Mrs. Alan L. Stein

Mr. and Mrs. Robert Swanson

Mr. and Mrs. Carter A. Thacher

Mr. and Mrs. Donovan Thayer

Mr. and Mrs. Brooks Walker, Jr.

Mrs. Anne MacDonald Walker

Mrs. Paul L. Wattis

Mr. and Mrs. Thomas W. Weisel

Mr. and Mrs. Alfred Wilsey

Mr. and Mrs. Michael Wilsey

Mr. and Mrs. William Wilson III

Staff

Mark Ashworth
Matting

Robert Barone
Communications Assistant

Graham W.J. Beal
Chief Curator

Oni Berglund
Collectors Forum Coordinator

Michael Berns
Membership Data Entry Operator

James Bernstein
*Codirector
Conservation Laboratory*

Margy Boyd
*Program Director
Art Tours and Travel*

Karen Brungardt
Library Assistant I

Beverly B. Buhnerkempe
Senior Assistant Controller

Catherine Byrne
Secretary, Development

Gail Camhi
Clerk Typist, Conservation

Eugenie Candau
Librarian

Hilda Cardenas
Admissions

Patti Carroll
*Curatorial Assistant
Department of Photography*

Neil Cockerline
Intern, Conservation

Van Deren Coke
*Director
Department of Photography*

Cynthia Coss
Bookshop Assistant

Lilly deGroot
Admissions

Robert Dix
Assistant Gallery Supervisor

Vera Anne Doherty
Receptionist

Diana du Pont
Research Assistant II

Robert Dziedzic
Bookshop Assistant

Inge-Lise Eckmann
*Codirector
Conservation Laboratory*

Debra Erviti
Slide Librarian

Kathleen Ferres
Curatorial Secretary

Cecilia Franklin
Controller

Helene Fried
*Coordinator, Department of
Architecture and Design*

Tina Garfinkel
Registrar/Exhibitions

Nona R. Ghent
Assistant Director, Operations

Greacian Goeke
*Assistant Director
Public Relations*

Donna Graves
Curatorial Assistant

Sarah Grew
Bookshop Assistant

Anita Gross
*Rights and Reproductions
Coordinator/Registration Secretary*

Miriam Grunfeld
Assistant Director of Education

Laurice Guerin
*Coordinator of Development and
Membership Services*

Phillip Hofstetter
Conservation Technician

Mindy Holdsworth
Registration Assistant I

Henry T. Hopkins
Director

Toby Kahn
*Director of Sales and Marketing
MuseumBooks*

Jane Kutzer
Bookshop Assistant

Debra Lande
Assistant Manager, MuseumBooks

Meredith Lee
Receptionist

Susan Lefkowich
*Assistant Director of Development
for Membership and Marketing*

Sara Leith
Research Assistant I

Robert Lieber
Bookshop Assistant

Susannah Marriner
Bookshop Assistant

T. William Melis
Deputy Director

JoAn Merle
Public Relations Secretary

Catherine Mills
Graphic Designer

Pauline Mohr
Conservator

Pamela Moore
Bookshop Assistant

Sarah Moulton
Public Relations Assistant I

Garna Muller
*Associate Director
Research/Collections*

Matrisha OnePerson
Bookshop Assistant

Kevin Osborne
Data Processing Coordinator

Pamela Pack
Associate Registrar

Elise M. Phillips
Manager, Modern Art Council

Steven Pon
Museum Technician

Kristy Pruett
Mail and Supplies Coordinator

Mary Rose Reade
Associate Director of Development

Suzanne Richards
Executive Secretary

Kent Roberts
Installation Supervisor

Nenita M. Rogers
Assistant Controller I

Carol Rosset
Registrar/Permanent Collection

Kathleen Rydar
Director of Development

Suzanne Sasaki
Bookshop Assistant

Michael Schwager
Curatorial Assistant

J. William Shank
Conservator

Myra Shapiro
Volunteer Coordinator

Joseph Shield
Gallery Attendant

Pamela Ann Siciliano-Lucido
*Administrative Secretary
Conservation Laboratory*

Carol Singer
Bookshop Assistant

Carol Stanton
Bookshop Assistant

Laura Sueoka
Research Assistant II

Sally Sutherland
*Assistant Director of Development
for Special Programs*

Beau Takahara
Education Department Coordinator

Cynthia Tanenbaum
Cashier

Lydia Tanji
Curatorial Secretary

Marcia Tanner
Director of Public Relations

Roy Tomlinson
Museum Technician

Carolyn Valdez
Admissions

Kay F. Van
Data Entry Operator

Dorothy Vandersteel
*Associate Curator
Department of Photography*

Karin Victoria
*Curatorial Secretary
Department of Photography*

Andrea Voinot
Bookshop Assistant

Ferd Von Schlafke
Preparator

David Wheeler
Museum Technician

Robert A. Whyte
Director of Education

James Wright
Conservator

San Francisco Museum of
Modern Art Rental Gallery

David Bedell
Preparator

Christina Henrikson
Corporate Consultant

Marian Parmenter
Director

Lauren Parrill
Office Manager

Photographs of the works of art have been supplied, in many cases, by the owners or custodians of the works, as cited in the Checklist of the Exhibition. The following list applies to photographs for which additional acknowledgment is due:

William H. Bengison: cat. no. 9; Courtesy John Berggruen: cat. no. 50; Courtesy Diane Brown Gallery: cat. nos. 3, 5; Geoffrey Clements: cat. no. 51; D. James Dee: fig. 5, cat. nos. 18, 19, 20, 45, 46; M. Lee Fatherree: cat. nos. 41, 42, 43; Rick Gardner: cat. nos. 38, 40; Courtesy Marian Goodman Gallery: cat. nos. 36, 37; Courtesy Martina Hamilton Gallery: cat. nos. 33, 34, 35; Scott Hyde: cat. no. 28; Peter Marcus: cat. nos. 11, 12, 13; Don Myer: cover; Phillips/Schwab: cat. nos. 47, 48; Eric Pollitzer: cat. no. 26; Courtesy Max Protetch Gallery: cat. nos. 7, 8, 46; George Rehsteiner: cat. no. 44; Earl Ripling: cat. nos. 14, 15, 16; Courtesy Sander Gallery: cat. nos. 30, 31, 32; Courtesy Sperone Westwater Gallery: cat. nos. 22, 25; Lee Stalsworth: cat. no. 17; Ivan van Dalla Tana: cat. no. 27; Zindman/Fremont: cat. nos. 21, 23, 24.